Perfect Phrases for Cover Letters

Michael Betrus

McGraw-Hill
New York Chicago San Francisco Lisbon
London Madrid Mexico City Milan New Delhi
San Juan Seoul Singapore Sydney Toronto

The **McGraw·Hill** Companies

1 2 3 4 5 6 7 8 9 0   FGR/FGR   0 9 8 7 6 5

ISBN 0-07-145406-3

 This book is printed on recycled, acid-free paper containing a minimum of 50% recycled, de-inked fiber.

McGraw-Hill books are available at special quantity discounts to use as premiums and sales promotions, or for use in corporate training programs. For more information, please write to the Director of Special Sales, Professional Publishing, McGraw-Hill, Two Penn Plaza, New York, NY 10121-2298. Or contact your local bookstore.

Table of Contents

Part I

Cover Letter Basics

Introduction

I hear it all the time as both a hiring manager and a career coach: "Cover letters? Résumés? That stuff is of the past. Now it's all about e-mail, job postings, and networking." I've interviewed hundreds of candidates for middle- and upper-level management for some giant firms, and this is what they tell me.

I interview candidates for six-figure jobs and some have absolutely horrendous résumés and cannot draft a well-written letter. I never understand it.

Now, some others do a great job on their letters and résumés. You know what? Simply because they have a well-written letter or résumé will get them recognized amidst a sea of responses that make *Mad* magazine (dating myself here) look like the *Wall Street Journal*. A great letter or résumé will get looked at just because it stands out.

My group has passed on some great candidates who have good pedigrees but such poorly written letters (e-mails, actually) or résumés that I cannot fathom them sending me a coherent weekly report.

Writing great letters and résumés is important because it is the first opportunity a recruiter or hiring manager gets to see an example of the work you can perform. If the résumé or letter has a typo or is not grammatically correct, that's not a great sign. I promise, I decline to meet with anyone that takes such little care.

This book will provide you with the best concept for cover letters, the consultative sales approach. This principle teaches you to spin your job search around the needs of the employer, not your skills or background. It will also provide you with many sample letters, letter formats, and guidelines, and thousands of phrases you can use when crafting that letter or e-mail to respond to an opportunity. Crafting a great letter or e-mail will get you noticed.

I have been involved in this type of work for years. In college, I wrote an article to help give my fellow college students at Michigan State University tips on getting hired when not pursuing the on-campus recruiting channel. As an accounting graduate, I had no more aptitude for getting published than anyone else. But even before I ever thought of writing that first book on résumés or cover letters, I did write effective cover letters and took a lot of time to spin my key messages around the needs of the employers.

Your attention to detail sends a message far beyond the words used in your response to a posting or a contact you are making through a colleague. Please pay attention to what you write! You will never know how many doors are closing because of imperfect writing; you just may not get the callbacks.

Formatting a Cover Letter and E-mail

I. Heading

To include name, address, phone number, fax number, e-mail, etc.

Patrick D. Dudash
1801 West Cortney Street
West Palm Beach, FL 33409
Phone: (561) 555-1234 / Fax: (561) 555-4321
Pdudash@xxx.com

The heading does not have to include all of the items listed here. Name, address, and telephone are critical, but fax number and e-mail address are optional. If you include your e-mail address, make sure you check it often. If you list a fax number, make sure you check it as well. And of all things, do not use your current employer's fax or e-mail address unless you have their approval.

E-mail note: You do not need to use this heading if you're sending an e-mail. Place this information at the signature line on an e-mail.

II. Date

September 5, 2006

E-mail note: You do not need to type in the date, since it will be time stamped anyway.

III. Name, Title, Company Name, and Address of Recipient

Ms. Maria Lane, Executive Vice President
PGR Industries, Inc.
1011 Dame Kate
Nashville, TN 23244

The only critical thing here is to make sure you include the company name and the recipient's title, if you know it.

E-mail note: Like the Heading, this is not required in an e-mail. However, in the "Subject" line in the e-mail, reference the specific position and recipient's name (if known). If you are responding to a Marketing Manager position, type in "Marketing Manager Candidate Dudash" in the subject line, to make it easier for the recipient to open and file and forward.

IV: Salutation

Dear Ms. Lane:

V. Power Introduction

Attention grabber—generating interest—why you are writing this employer.

Over the last few months I've noticed your firm moving into consulting with several health-care firms. After speaking with Mike Kiryn, I am aware that you are bidding on the upcoming opening of two new Columbia hospitals. You will no doubt need significant health-care industry expertise to drive this account. Health care can really get complicated when trying to balance aggressive marketing and sales techniques along with a more public entity image.

I have been working in marketing and public relations for nine years, most recently with Humana in Florida. We successfully opened 11 new hospitals over the last six years, and even experienced a storm when we opened the one in Orlando. That one opened in the midst of a major citywide controversy about the rising cost of health care, and much criticism was directed our way in the media. Under my direction, Humana successfully overcame that encounter and now that hospital is one of the most successful in the region.

Notice how the letter opens giving Ms. Lane an understanding that the applicant knows her business, and then ties her needs into Mr. Dudash's background.

VI. Purpose of the Letter

After working with Humana for several years, I feel I need a change. I have informed our regional director that I will be relocating to the Northeast, and would like to move into the consulting arena, supporting the health-care industry. After 15 years in the industry in key public relations roles, and after seeing the explosion in the industry with too many green managers making fundamental mistakes, I know I can share a wealth of knowledge to improve their operations. As well, I have many key contacts in the industry, but am not interested in starting up a consulting operation of my own. I can provide a solid lead list to broaden your client list.

VII. Critical Messages

I offer your consulting service the following skills:
- 15 years in public relations
- 15 years in the health-care industry
- Expertise in new launches and crisis management
- Key contacts within the industry

IX. Call to Action

You must initiate the next steps.

Please expect my telephone call in the next week so that we might be able to set a time to meet and discuss employment possibilities that would serve our mutual interests.

X. Close

Thanks for your consideration. I look forward to meeting with you soon.

Sincerely,
Patrick Dudash

As with any letter, you can use a block style paragraph format (shown here) or indent the first line. Both are equally acceptable, though the block style is used more in business.

Cover Letter Basics

This letter does a comprehensive job of illustrating the way to draw the connection between the applicant's skills and the company's needs. Even in e-mail format, it works brilliantly.

Broadcast Letters

The broadcast letter is a hybrid between a résumé and cover letter and coveys much of your credentials without a résumé.

The broadcast letter looks more like a letter than a résumé, so the reader may be apt to give it more attention. This is especially true when a screening authority—a Human Resources recruiter or administrative assistant—is screening candidates. They may be more apt to pass on a "letter" to the boss but might more readily redirect a "résumé" to Personnel or Human Resources.

Suppose you're employed but do not want to take any chances that your current employer might find out you are looking for a job. Certainly you will not want to send out a résumé that names your current employer. This would be a good time to consider creating a broadcast letter.

The broadcast letter may offer less information than your résumé, but can hold more sizzle. More so than a résumé, it is an exercise in creativity, and it needs to be written very well or the strategy can backfire and not be advantageous.

Most broadcast letters today are sent in e-mail form and therefore need to contain short paragraphs and use bullets for key points. You need to keep them short and powerful in the introductions and in the closing.

Sample Introductions

Dear Mr. Grant:

Maria Lane provided me with your name and thought it might be beneficial if we got together and discussed your medical research program.

I set up the medical research program at the UNC, and today, 10 years after its inception, the program is considered one of the best in the country. I would like to make your program the benchmark for all others to emulate. Below are a few career highlights:

[Career highlights in bullet form follow.]

Dear Mr. Connors:

Paul Anners, probation officer for Hillsborough County, gave me your name and suggested I call you. I am a highly experienced locksmith, and though I have no formal training, there is very little I don't know about the business. In fact, I am working with Paul because I became too good at my trade.

Paul told me that you work with people who have experienced some trouble with the law ONLY if they are committed to total rehabilitation and work hard to get ahead. I have a wife and three children. I made a horrific mistake two years ago and will never do anything to jeopardize my future again.

I offer you the following:

[Career highlights in bullet form follow.]

Cover Letter Basics

Dear Mr. Regal:

I spearheaded the successful turnaround of three Fortune 100 companies and nine nationally recognized firms since 1981. Though my name is not a household word nor have I been CEO, COO, or president of any of the organizations that I have helped rehabilitate, I have been the strategic financial tactician behind some of the most successful reengineering efforts in the past quarter century in high-tech environments.

Your executive recruiting firm is recognized worldwide as the leader in helping top corporations secure visionary leaders and senior-level executives. Following 17 years of consultative prominence with three of the nation's leading consulting firms, I would like now to identify a company that would be interested in my leadership qualities on a long-term basis in a top position as President, CEO, COO, or CFO.

[Career highlights in bullet form follow.]

Dear Mr. Louega:

A few months ago, I completed the sale of Thurner Industries, Inc., a company that, in four years of leadership, I successfully turned into a highly profitable and much desired operation. Although I have been offered a similar role for another subsidiary of Thurner Industries, I would like to explore career opportunities building technology-based organizations. In anticipation of opportunities you may have for a Senior Operations or Manufacturing Executive, I enclose my résumé for your consideration. Recent accomplishments include:

[Career highlights in bullet form follow.]

Dear Ms. Lourdes:

If your staff could benefit through the addition of an eminently qualified senior sales professional, then I suggest it could prove to our mutual benefit to establish a dialogue. While secure in my present post, I am confidentially exploring new opportunities to which I could increase my span of control and have a greater contribution to overall sales results.

As my background reflects, my track record of performance demonstrates consistent advancement in the sales field over the past 14 years within the high-tech and prototype manufacturing environments. Of specific note may be the following indicators of the sales results I've produced for my employers:

[Career highlights in bullet form follow.]

Dear Mr. Kroll:

As a medical/pharmaceutical account manager and area trainer, managing a $5.5 million New York metro-region territory, I offer quantifiable expertise directly related to an 18-year background with Beecham Laboratories, a Fortune 200 leader in health care solutions.

In recent years, I have produced over $18 million in sales in only 48 months, have attained three Beecham "Quota Buster" awards, and have been appointed to Beecham's prestigious "Presidential Team." Customers appreciate my extensive product knowledge, training abilities, and thorough follow-up. Beecham has recognized my creative marketing, innovative product launches, and comprehensive new-hire mentoring.

Representative accomplishments in specific medical/pharmaceutical areas include:

(Career highlights in bullet form follow.)

Dear Ms. Siegal:

As current Vice President of Finance for a Fortune 500 industrial leader, and former CFO of two mid-sized manufacturers, I have been instrumental in the origination of highly imaginative and highly profitable financial management programs achieved through motivational leadership blended with sound financing and creative thinking.

The following accomplishments reflect the absolute value that I can bring to Cerion's current and long-term business ventures:

[Career highlights in bullet form follow.]

Dear Mr. Dixon:

Recognized as a dynamic management executive, I possess a career in successfully building and leading companies to profitability and growth. My expertise includes new business development, strategic sales and marketing campaigns, team leadership and operational management.

- For the past three years, I have served as …
- I was recruited to plan and implement an aggressive sales and marketing plan to establish worldwide sales and …
- Prior, I served as the Vice President, Sales and Marketing for …

Closing Phrases

- I would like to stop by and introduce myself and share my portfolio with you. Would next week be convenient? I will contact you this Thursday at 11:00 A.M. to determine if such arrangements would interest you. Thank you for your time and consideration.

- If you believe, as I do, that my qualifications and credentials merit further review on how I can best serve your community center's cultural needs, I would appreciate the opportunity of meeting with you. Please expect my telephone call in the coming week to arrange such a meeting. Thank you for your consideration.

- I will be meeting with Janine next Monday at 10:00 A.M. and will plan to call you from her office. If you need any further information about me, she suggested you call her at (555) 555-5678. I thank you for your time and trust in Janine and me. I will not let you down!

- As a follow-up to this correspondence, I will call you next week to determine if my qualifications meet your needs at this time. As I have not yet discussed my plans with Thurner, I would appreciate your discretion in this matter.

- If you are looking for a senior manager who will make an immediate and positive impact upon operations, revenue streams, and profit margins, I would like to explore the opportunity. I look forward to speaking with you soon.

Consultative Sales Approach

Marketing principles revolve around the four Ps: product, place, promotion, and price. Your self-marketing principles should revolve around the same principles. Thus, it makes sense to draw the parallels even further.

Marketers attempt to create and position a product to meet the needs of their target sales segment. You should position yourself in a manner that meets the needs of your targeted employers. Once marketing does its thing, it is up to sales to complete the process. This is the place—the distribution element of the marketing mix. Your sales element is in full force when you are in the interviewing stage, but even before that you need to set up the stage for a strong sell.

Enter consultative sales, which requires you to understand the needs of the customer (or your prospective employer) and sell the customer on the idea that you have a product to meet those needs. To rise above the pack in the job search process, you need to demonstrate to the prospective employer that you clearly understand its needs and you can fill the gap in its organization to meet those needs.

Here are a few examples of things to look for in an organization. You should understand and research them before beginning the process of writing the cover letter and sending your résumé so you can address those items in your communications, just as in sales and marketing.

- Existing products
- New products
- Geographic presence
- Climate of the industry
- Competitive products and companies
- Emerging trends in the industry and within the organization
- Profile of the current staff
- Profile of the desired staff skill set
- The company's key business or market drivers

There are many others, but you get the point. You need to learn about these things. Then you can better position yourself as someone who can help the company achieve its goals, rather than someone who needs a job. The research should take place before you send the cover letter and résumé so that you can customize them to meet the needs you uncovered.

You can learn about these things in several ways. When you have uncovered that information, you can use it in two ways. In your résumé you should position, spin, or highlight your accomplishments to make them consistent with the company's overall goals. Your cover letter is the vehicle to address what you've learned and how you can help them meet their goals.

The Formula

Here is the basic formula for a consultative cover letter:

PART 1. Based on research you've completed, this first section of the letter is where you state the needs of the company or hiring manager. The purpose is to demonstrate your understanding of their situation and business. If nothing else, it shows the reader you know something about his or her situation and needs.

PART 2. This is the bridge. Draw the connection between what the business's needs are and how its people resources address them. You can see multiple examples of this on the following pages.

PART 3. Now you begin to present information about yourself. You've stated the company's needs and how people will meet those needs. Now you need to connect yourself to the solution. Write just a couple statements about how your skills and accomplishments will solve the company's problems and meet its needs.

Take a look at the sample letters section and look for the ways each letter opens, demonstrating an understanding of where the company is and where it is going. Then look for the way the writers are connecting the company's needs with their skills. If you can master this concept, you will be successful not just in your job search, but also in your overall career.

Opening Phrases

- Lisa Councilman provided me with your name and suggested I contact you regarding summer employment this season. Apparently, Lisa has worked for you for the past three summers, but she will be in Europe this year and thought I might work in her place.

- After completing much research on [prospective employer] the industry over the last few months, it has become apparent that [your company] holds a unique position in the market.
- Your marketing director, Jeff Kilpatrick, mentioned you are looking for an MIS director. He told me some very interesting things about GB and I am impressed, not only with the growth and profitability, but in the similarities between GB and Diversified Centers, my current employer. GB has added 23 new training centers in the U.S. With that much widespread activity, MIS needs must surely be exploding.
- Melissa Sumner at Touchstone recently informed me that you are overseeing costumes and makeup for the new film, "The Nutty Professor". Melissa shared with me some of the effects that you are planning to use to transform the lead character between the thin professor and the very overweight professor. In order to pull this off, you will undoubtedly need artists skilled in this field.
- Over the last few months I've noticed your firm moving into consulting with several health-care firms. After speaking with Patrick Workley, I am aware you are bidding on the upcoming opening of two new Columbia hospitals. You will no doubt need significant health-care industry expertise to drive this account …
- I have been researching HP and their play in the integrated services offerings for some time. I was intrigued to read about the upcoming VoiP announcement that is currently scheduled for this fall. VoiP is reportedly going to converge data and voice transport products into a single, more cost-

effective transport that can support virtually unlimited bandwidth demands.

■ The *Chicago Times* ran an article last month indicating UPS was expanding its call center operations in the Chicago area and that a benchmarking effort was going to be made to bring the center back in-house after many years of contracting the service. Now that the talk of strike has been put to bed, I am sure you will be focusing attention again on this project. I believe I can help!

Middle Section Phrases

■ In order to meet your aggressive growth goals of launching this market by next fall, you will certainly need a strong RF team that has experience in the CDMA platform. Specifically, you will need a team that has experience optimizing the Lucent and Nortel base stations. As a consultant, I …

■ With that much national activity, you must need each site to be networked with your home office for both voice and data transport, as well as establish a WAN to improve real-time connectivity. As well, the design aspect of the business must eat up a lot of bandwidth in data transport, so it would surely help if you could share information more quickly and efficiently, while maintaining your privacy firewall.

■ Experience with plastics, makeup, special wraps, and the various maskings take a great deal of skill to apply in a way that is transparent to the viewer. I know; I was the lead artist for several movies and clips, including Michael

Jackson's *Thriller* video, *Halloween H20*, and in several *Tales from the Crypt* episodes.

■ In order to pull this off, you will surely need to have strong relationships in place with the CLECs or ILECs in given markets. For in the short run that is the only way you can provide the local access "last mile." I have a lot of experience working with Bell Atlantic/Nynex and Bell South in xDSL …

■ Some of my career highlights include the following, which actually tie in closely with the emerging needs at UPS:

> Personnel management and team-building; directing a team to consistently exceed organizational expectations

> Systems and operational benchmarking; developing systems of operations that can be replicated in other operations

> A highly competitive but jovial manager who inspires success and while demanding results

> Strong finance/budget management skills; bottom-line oriented

■ I understand you are looking for people who have experience in retail environments, are customer service oriented, are loyal and dependable, have working knowledge of point-of-sales computer technologies, and are drug free. Retail environments like this can be so difficult to find good people. I am in my third year at UCLA majoring in Business Administration and have five years retail experience (The Body Shop, Wolfe Camera, and The Gap) and am very familiar with POS computer systems.

Closing Phrases

- My experience appears to be in perfect line with your needs right now and what you will need after launch. I will give you a call next week to set up some time for us to talk further.
- It appears that my accomplishments with Diversified Centers are in line with your MIS needs at GB. I will give you a call next week to set up a meeting to talk further.
- My experience is very consistent with what you will need for your upcoming film. Please review my attached résumé for the specifics of my film credits. You will see that I would be a good fit for helping you with all of the makeup and related preparations for the demanding transformation scenes. I will call you next Tuesday and set up a time to stop by the studio to meet you.
- I am sure that you see connection between my five areas of strength above and the criteria by which UPS evaluates potential managers. I know your time is extremely valuable, and so is mine. Therefore I would enjoy speaking with you for a few moments over the telephone to determine if an in-person meeting might be beneficial to us both. Please expect my call next Monday afternoon. If this is not a good time to chat for a few minutes, we can arrange another time that is mutually convenient.
- Bob mentioned that you are presently looking for a retail manager to direct operations at your flagship location. I

would be interested in meeting with you to discuss this exciting opportunity. I have one more week to finish up things with FSS and then I am available to meet with you in Nashville. I will call you tomorrow to discuss this fax.

- I will be off for the summer as of May 29. However, I will be home for spring break (April 7-15) and would like to stop by and introduce myself to you. We can both be sure that Maria would not have introduced us to each other if she didn't feel I could fill her shoes in a way that measures up to your high standards.

Consultative Approach Cover Letters

MELISSA SUMNER
9981 Southern Boulevard, West Palm Beach, Florida 33409
(561) 555-5719

March 29, 20__
Ms. Theresa Mascagni
Vice President Technical Operations
4800 Oakland Park Boulevard
Fort Lauderdale, FL 33341

Dear Ms. Mascagni:

After completing much research on the wireless communications industry over the last few months, it has become apparent that NextWave holds a unique position in the market. NextWave has secured multiple C-Block licenses across the country and when built out will have a national presence comparable to AT&T and Sprint.

In order to meet your aggressive growth goals of launching this market by next fall, you will certainly need a strong RF team that has experience in the CDMA platform. Specifically, you will need a team that has experience optimizing the Lucent and Nortel base stations.

As a consultant, I led RF teams from network design to launch with both PrimeCo and Sprint PCS in the Chicago and Dallas MTAs, both of which were on a Lucent platform. I can provide excellent references from both. I think NextWave is a cutting-edge operation, one in which ingenuity, creativity, and drive can make a material impression. I want to be a part of your team.

My experience is in perfect line with your needs right now and what you will need after launch. I will give you a call next week to set up some time for us to talk further.

Sincerely,
Melissa Sumner

GLENNA HAZEN
2357 Golf Drive Lane, Coppell, TX 75220
(817) 555-5974

June 9, 20___
Mr. Grant D. Powers
CEO Golden Bear International
Golden Bear Plaza
11712 U.S. Highway 1
North Palm Beach, FL 33412

Dear Mr. Powers:

Your Controller, Mr. Gerald Haverhill, told me over golf a few weeks ago that you are looking for an MIS director. He told me some very interesting things about GB, and I was impressed, not only with the growth and profitability, but with the similarities between GB and Diversified Centers, my current employer. GB has added 23 new training centers in the U.S., as well as overseen the design of all Jack Nicklaus courses. With that much widespread activity, MIS needs must surely be exploding.

With that level of national activity, you must need each site to be networked with your home office for both voice and data transport, as well as establish a WAN to improve real-time connectivity. As well, the design aspect of the business must eat up a lot of bandwidth in data transport, so it would surely help if you could share information more quickly and efficiently, while maintaining your privacy firewall. My current operation is quite similar. I have built a very efficient network for our many regional locations to communicate. Diversified Centers builds and manages strip mall shopping centers for Tom Thumb grocery stores. Our network enables each regional office to stay in touch via e-mail and shared drives through our WAN, as well as utilize the Sprint ION network for real-time communications of high bandwidth development plans, similar to your use of golf course designs.

It appears that my accomplishments with Diversified Centers is in line with your MIS needs at GB. I will give you a call next week to set up a meeting to talk further.

Looking forward to meeting you,
Glenna Hazen

P.S. Gerald told me you are quite close with Mr. Nicklaus. Please congratulate him on his fine Masters showing!

CAROLYN KELLENBURGER
5534 College Parkway
Cape Coral, FL 33410
(941) 555-9753

March 15, 20__
Ms. Kimberly Houston
Paramount Pictures
4800 Hollywood Boulevard
Santa Monica, CA 90211

Dear Ms. Houston:

Jim Talley at Touchstone recently informed me that you are overseeing costumes and makeup for the new film *The Nutty Professor*. Jim shared with me some of the effects that you are planning to use to transform the lead character between the thin professor and the very overweight professor. In order to pull this off, you will undoubtedly need artists skilled in this field.

Experience with plastics, makeup, special wraps, and the various maskings takes a great deal of skill to apply in a way that is transparent to the viewer. I know; I was the lead artist for several movies and clips, including Michael Jackson's *Thriller* video, *Halloween H20* and several *Tales from the Crypt* episodes.

My experience is very consistent with what you will need for your upcoming film.

Please review my attached résumé for the specifics of my film credits. You will see that I would be a good fit for helping you with all of the makeup and related preparations for the demanding transformation scenes. I will call you next Tuesday and set up a time to stop by the studio to meet you.

Sincerely,
Carolyn Kellenburger

MISTI DEORNELLAS
45227 Michigan Avenue, Chicago, IL 64197
(312) 555-3125

March 9, 1999
Ms. Maria Lane, Executive Vice President
Hyde and Smithson Public Relations, Inc.
1800 Scenic Way
Mountain View, VT 19877

Dear Ms. Lane:

Over the last few months I've noticed your firm moving into consulting with several health-care firms. After speaking with Tom Aimee, I am aware that you are bidding on the upcoming opening of two new Columbia hospitals. You will no doubt need significant health-care industry expertise to drive this account.

Health care can really get complicated when trying to balance aggressive marketing and sales techniques along with a more public entity image.

The two new locations in Portsmouth and Springfield will be delicate openings given the amount of bad press Columbia has received in the last year or two.

Columbia has been in trouble with both the IRS and the FBI for tampering with federal aid and overbilling Medicare. They will undoubtably need good advice on how to position their openings to get off on the right foot.

I have been working in marketing and public relations for nine years, most recently with Humana in Florida. We successfully opened 11 new hospitals over the last six years, and even experienced a storm when we opened the one in Orlando.

That one opened in the midst of a major citywide controversy regarding the for-profit nature of Humana versus the for-the-good-of-the-people persona hospitals have maintained. Under my direction Humana successfully overcame that encounter, and now that hospital is one of the most successful in the region.

My skills are very much in line with the needs of both your firm and your clients:

- 15 years in public relations
- 15 years in the health-care industry
- Expertise in new launches and crisis management
- Key contacts within the industry

Please expect my telephone call in the next week so that we might be able to set a time to meet and discuss employment possibilities that would serve our mutual interests.

Sincerely,
Misti DeOrnellas

WALT JOHNSON
2357 Indiana Lane
Indianapolis, Indiana 49877
(317) 555-5687

September 8, 20__
Ms. Christy Garcia
Director Sales and Marketing
AT&T Data Services
3333 Westwood One
Indianapolis, IN 49557

Dear Ms. Garcia:

I have been researching AT&T and their play in the integrated services offerings for some time. I was intrigued to read about the upcoming INC announcement that is currently scheduled for this fall. INC is reportedly going to converge data and voice transport products into a single, more cost-effective transport that can support virtually unlimited bandwidth demands.

In order to pull this off, you will surely need to have strong relationships in place with the CLECs or ILECs in given markets. In the short run that is the only way you can provide the local access "last mile." I have a lot of experience working with Bell Atlantic/Nynex and Bell South in xDSL. Surely xDSL will be your plan for last mile access when it is built out, and you will need skilled network data engineers to optimize and design that integration.

Please take a look at my résumé, which reflects the broad experience I have developed in data transport and xDSL technology. I will call you next week for an appointment when we can review this further.

Sincerely,
Walt Johnson

CHARLENE W. PARKER
668 West Hannover Boulevard, Chicago, IL 60623
Phone: (773) 555-2486
E-mail: Fivestar10@Main.net

July 9, 20___
Mrs. Grace Billings, Customer Service Manager
United Parcel Service
1000 State Street
Chicago, IL 60602

Dear Mrs. Billings:

Congratulations on the recent contract between the pilot's union and management. The recent strike was surely devastating, not only to UPS, but the nation as a whole who depend on and trust UPS. The agreement signed last week ensures that the good name of and extraordinary service provided by UPS will not be tarnished.

I read in the Business section of the *Chicago Times,* over a month ago, that UPS was expanding its call center operations in the Chicago area and that a benchmarking effort was going to be made to bring the center back in-house after many years of contracting the service. Now that the talk of a strike has been put to bed, I am sure you will be focusing attention again on this project. I believe I can help!

I work as a Call Center Manager for Sears Roebuck and Company here in Chicago. They too once contracted out their call center/customer service operations and made the decision to bring it in-house six years ago. I was one of nine team leaders responsible for the strategic planning and implementation of the conversion from contracted to in-house call center operations for Sears.

Some of my career highlights include the following, which actually tie in closely with the emerging needs at UPS:

- Personnel management and team building; directing a team to consistently exceed organizational expectations
- Systems and operational benchmarking; developing systems of operations that can be replicated in other operations
- A highly competitive but jovial manager who inspires success while demanding results
- Strong finance/budget management skills; bottom-line oriented

I am sure that you see the connection between my four areas of strength above and the criteria by which UPS evaluates potential managers. I know your time is extremely valuable, and so is mine.

Therefore, I would enjoy speaking with you for a few moments over the telephone to determine if an in-person meeting might be beneficial to us both.

Please expect my call next Monday afternoon. If this is not a good time to chat for a few minutes, we can arrange another time that is mutually convenient.

Thank you for your time and consideration.

Sincerely,
Charlene W. Parker

CYNTHIA E. GOODMAN
2121 East 75th Street, Fort Lauderdale, FL 33304
(954) 555-5945

March 21, 20__
Mr. Howard Finelaw, President
Valet Services of South Florida
9205 Dixie Highway, Suite 200-B
Pompano Beach, FL 33360

Dear Mr. Finelaw:

Our paths have met on at least two occasions, and I was truly impressed each time. Please allow me to explain. I attended the Executive Women's Association gala event three weeks ago at the Cypress Creek Marriott, where more than 400 people attended. When I drove my car to the valet, I was awestruck by the professionalism of the attendants, the uniforms, and the courtesies extended, not only to me, but to everyone. I mean to say that the valet service was so exceptional, it was the talk of the evening!

When I asked to speak to the hotel manager to rave about the valet service, he told me that it had nothing to do with the Marriott. I found out that your company is responsible for this level of service. Last Saturday night my wife and I went to the Kravis Center to see *Phantom of the Opera*. Needless to say, half of South Florida was there—and so were you! Again, I could not believe the level of service provided—simply exceptional.

So our paths have met on two occasions over the past four to five weeks—and I'd like to propose a third. I am a highly successful sales professional, and I will represent only companies with top-rated products and services. I would like to propose a meeting to discuss how I can best help your company grow and prosper even beyond the success you have had to this point.

After completing some research online, I discovered your Web site. I noticed that your company has plans to expand into Broward and Martin Counties. I know I can use my plethora of corporate contacts to help you build your company. And if you decide you want to go regional, state, or national, I have the experience and verifiable track record to assist in this area as well.

And here's the best part—I enjoy being compensated for results, and I guarantee results. I do not require a high base salary compensation plan, but actually prefer an attractive commission program. I am a six-figure earner and am compensated only when I bring in the business. My past sales experience has been focused on hospitality oriented business, so I have key contacts with companies that can use professional valet services. In fact, I have spent the last three evenings studying the valet business and have familiarized myself with the competition, past and future trends, and growth/profit potential. Based on my preliminary findings, you are in a niche market with almost unlimited potential.

I have enclosed a detailed résumé of my qualifications and will contact you early next week to discuss possible scenarios for future employment with your company.

Thanks for taking the time to read this letter. I do hope we can meet in the next week or so.

Sincerely,
Cynthia E. Goodman

HELEN R. HENDERSON
21 Village Street
San Francisco, CA 99465
(302) 555-6102

February 22, 20___
Ms. Alice Greene
Center Plaza Hallmark
201 Broadway, Center Plaza
San Francisco, CA 99427

Dear Ms. Greene:

Bonnie Taylor provided me with your name and suggested I contact you regarding summer employment this season. Apparently, Bonnie has worked for you for the past three summers but will be in Europe this year and thought I might work in her place.

I understand you are looking for people who have experience in retail environments, are customer service oriented, are loyal and dependable, have working knowledge of point-of-sales computer technologies, and are drug free. In retail environments like this it can be so difficult to find good people. The retail stores I have worked with at school have really struggled to get good, bright, and courteous people on staff.

I am in my third year at UCLA, majoring in Business Administration. As well, I have five years of retail experience (The Body Shop, Wolfe Camera, and The Gap) and am very familiar with POS computer systems.

I will be off for the summer as of May 29. However, I will be home for spring break (April 7–15) and would like to stop by and introduce myself to you. We can both be sure that Bonnie would not have introduced us to each other if she didn't feel I could fill her shoes in a way that measures up to your high standards.

I will call you next week to see if we can arrange an interview during my spring break. Thanks in advance for your consideration.

Sincerely,
Helen R. Henderson

Sample Letters for All Occations

Letter Targeting a Specific Employer

PAULINA TAYLOR

June 4, 20__

Patti Coury
PCR Firm
Los Angeles, CA 90211

Dear Ms. Coury:

After contributing to the growth and success of AMEX Financial Services for 12 years, I am seeking new challenges with an enterprising company in need of someone with exceptional planning, leadership, and analytical qualities. One of your colleagues, Bill Stephens, and I met for lunch earlier this week, and Bill recommended that I contact you regarding prospective opportunities in your department.

As evidenced in the enclosed résumé, my experience encompasses all aspects of corporate business development and operations, strategic planning, budget administration, systems integration, internal management consulting, resource utilization, and project management. My ability to analyze needs and develop unique programs designed to yield a profitable outcome has proven to be one of my greatest assets.

Credited with significantly impacting bottom-line profitability and reducing operational costs at AMEX Financial, I excel at modeling complex situations in order to generate investment/costing details for new business ventures. I am technologically proficient, with direct experience in remittance, imaging, and systems design and development. My record of achievements is exemplary, as I have successfully directed and managed complex assignments while meeting or exceeding anticipated scheduling and budgetary projections.

Characterized by others as visionary and decisive, I possess keen instincts and offer strategies to quickly effect change and improvement. I am equally at ease working as a team member or independently, and enjoy a leadership role where I can foster motivational and mentoring relationships with colleagues and subordinates.

I am most interested in an opportunity where I can provide strong corporate leadership and vision. I would welcome the chance to discuss with you personally the value I offer Hamilton Company. If you feel such a discussion would be beneficial, please contact me at (310) 555-1212.

Sincerely,
Patti Coury

Broadcast Letter Samples (Sent as E-mail)

Dear Mrs. Curri:

I have a solid record for bringing in advertising dollars to prestigious, upscale publications from Aspen, Beverly Hills, and Palm Beach, to Newport, Rhode Island, and San Diego. As a top producing sales professional, I am certain I can be a contributing member of your advertising sales team.

Key Strengths:

- Presentation and closing skills
- Networking; building key alliances
- Graphic art and production management
- Concept development
- Customer service & retention management
- High ethical/professional standards

Past Employment (1990-2005):

Aspen Monthly, Aspen, CO	Sales Supervisor
Beverly Hills Illustrated, Beverly Hills, CA	Sales Associate
The LaJolla Magazine, San Diego, CA	Sales Associate
Palm Beach Illustrated, Palm Beach, FL	Advertising Sales Associate
The Newport News, Newport, RI	Sales Associate

I would like to stop by and introduce myself and share my portfolio to you. Would next week be convenient? I will contact you this Thursday at 11:00 A.M. to determine if such arrangements interest you.

Thank you for your time and consideration.

Sincerely,
Stephen Kayl

August 2, 20__
Mr. Holland L. Regal, President
Beltway Technologies, Ltd.
6300 Hunter Way
Waltham, MA 12197

Dear Mr. Regal:

I spearheaded the successful turnaround of three Fortune 100 companies and nine nationally recognized firms since 1981. Though my name is not a household word nor have I been CEO, COO, or president of any of the organizations that I have helped rehabilitate, I have been the strategic financial tactician behind some of the most successful reengineering efforts in the past quarter century in high-tech environments.

Your executive recruiting firm is recognized worldwide as the leader in helping top corporations secure visionary leaders and senior-level executives. Following 17 years of consultative prominence with three of the nation's leading consulting firms, I would like now to identify a company that would be interested in my leadership qualities on a long-term basis in a top position as President, CEO, COO, or CFO.

Three employers over the past 17 years:

1. Arthur Anderson
2. Mackenzie & Associates
3. Corporate Dynamics International

Twelve notable client companies (accompanied by outstanding references) that I have consulted for:

1. General Electric
2. Hewlett Packard
3. Cisco Systems
4. Compaq Computer
5. Intel
6. Softkey International
7. GBC
8. Digital Equipment
9. Delta Airlines
10. Lucent Technologies
11. LaserTools, Inc.
12. Ford Motor Company

My educational qualifications:

MBA Stanford University, 1980

Bachelor of Science: Industrial Engineering/Business Management, Tufts University

Faculty Staff Member: Peter Drucker Worldwide Training and Educational Academy

Maximizing shareholder earnings/growth management/ financial integrity:

These are the three critical strengths I bring to the table. I am well-connected with Wall Street and have been personally involved with positioning three companies in the past four years to go public (including drafting a 230-page financial summary and pro forma). Finally, I have spent 60 percent of my time over the last five years in the international, global arena—helping position companies to maximize foreign market potential.

Certainly I do not want to waste precious time for either of us. Should you feel that you might come across a client seeking executive-level leadership that could take advantage of my qualifications and verifiable track record, feel free to contact me and I will forward a detailed, highly confidential résumé with supporting documentation. I would be seeking a position with a minimum compensation package of $200,000 and equity stock options based on performance.

Thank you for taking the time to review this letter. I look forward to hearing back from you if you feel an opportunity might exist that would benefit one of your client companies.

Sincerely,
Cliff W. O'Brien

Networking Letter Samples

NIKA NIKSIRAT
215 Hartman Drive, Portsmouth, NH 03801
(603) 555-4606

June 2, 20___

Mr. Benjamin Chang
Technical Director, Cisco Systems
4399 Central Avenue
Boston, MA 18002

Dear Mr. Chang:

Dave Tinker from Cellcorp suggested I contact you. He said you "know more about the network router business than anyone this side of the Mason-Dixon line." I knew you would be someone I had to meet.

Though I am employed with Bell Atlantic, I have decided to make a career move toward a more entrepreneurial upstart operation. I am not writing you for a position, but rather to get some industry advice from you. Companies that are just starting out are usually well capitalized but may be short on technical or operational expertise.

Having been involved with several major product launches with Bell Atlantic, I feel I have been through it all. However, going forward I think I can make a greater impact with a start-up. A start-up will be able to utilize my experience, and it could be a good situation for them and me.

I will call you next week to talk to you for a few minutes. Don't worry, I only want some advice, and if you have the time, I would love to take you to lunch. Thanks in advance for all your time!

Sincerely,
Nika Niksirat

DEBBIE McMULLAN
1215 Phillips Drive
New York, NY 10001
(212) 555-9555

December 3, 20__

Ms. Beth Pasterz
Robert Half International
1222 Park Avenue
New York, NY 10012

Dear Ms. Pasterz:

Thanks for speaking with me on the phone earlier. I agree that there probably isn't a good match between me and your current positions to fill. However, you did mention that based on our phone interview you thought my credentials were strong, and it got me thinking.

Would you still mind if we met? I am new to the New York area, as my husband was just transferred, and it looks like we'll be here for quite a while. You seemed to be fairly well connected and in the know as to what's going on here. I would love to meet just to get your advice on which firms I might avoid, which might be good, and what the overall climate is like in New York.

I realize you are probably quite busy, and I'd be happy to buy you breakfast or lunch just to talk for a few minutes. I promise I won't monopolize your time. You never know, maybe I will be calling you soon to help me recruit my new accounting staff.

I will call you on Friday and try to set something up. Thanks, I really enjoyed talking with you today.

Best Regards,
Debbie McMullan

Internet Job Posting Responses

I have some friends that have posted for dozens of positions over the Internet, on sites like careerbuilder.com or monster.com, never getting one response.

Here is what happens on the other side, speaking from my personal experience. Hiring managers or recruiters get so many unqualified responses that they give very little time to any one résumé or letter. Letters never get read, by me anyway, if they are more than three lines per paragraph and appear not to be germane to the position applied.

Internet Job Posting Letter Tips

1. Short paragraphs, no more than three lines.
2. Hard space returns so the layout is broken up on the viewer's page.
3. Relevance! The letters should closely align to the job requirements.
4. Bullets: easier to read and to the point.

An ineffective letter is much worse than no letter. Below are some phrases that will help you respond to Internet job postings. Look at this for structure and layout, not the actual words.

With e-mail letters and Internet postings, structure has as much to do with the letter effectiveness as the letter.

Internet Posting Letter Response Structure

1. Quick reference to job you are applying.
2. Three to four bullets summarizing why you are the right candidate. These should absolutely mirror the posting's job requirements.
3. Quick, nonwordy closing.

Dear Microsoft:

I am very interested in speaking with you about your national accounts position, as it is described as a perfect fit for my experience.

I do offer [and then list their position criteria spun around your career highlights]:

- Ten years experience in national account sales targeting Fortune 500 accounts
- Nine years training and development experience
- Consultative sales approach
- Negotiating, RFP and RFQ expertise

Please see my professional career highlights on my résumé below.

As a team member of your organization, I can provide:

- Effective applications solutions for financial and business operations

- Analysis, needs determination, and project management
- Powerful team leadership
- Technical instruction and business support for end-users and clients on business issues and application implementation

My enclosed résumé clearly shows I have qualifying skills and abilities compatible with this position. Briefly, they are:

- Considerable industry-related experience augmented by a formal education and refined by specialized training
- A proven record of success achieved through diligence, hard work, attention to detail, and my belief in a consistent application of the fundamentals
- A sincere desire to contribute to the continued growth and success of your company

After you have the opportunity to review my résumé, I would like to meet with you to discuss how effectively I can contribute. Should you have any questions before scheduling an appointment I may be reached through the number listed above.

Tips

Cover Letter and E-mail Tips

NO TYPOS! You would be shocked how many typos still exist in letters and especially e-mails today. Sometimes I will review letters and e-mails of very experienced professionals and think, "You have got to be kidding me," when I see so many typos. If I were to guide you to avoid typos, it may not mean the same thing to you it does to me. Here are some specific things to watch for that I see all the time:

- Randomly capitalized words in sentences or phrases. If it is not a proper noun or the beginning of a sentence, it doesn't get capitalized. You should not use capitalization just because you want to add punch.
- Spaces after commas and periods. You need to have them.
- Long, run-on sentences. Look, I'm no Stephen King when it comes to creative writing, or effective writing either. But I do understand that short sentences are more powerful than long ones. In long sentences the point gets lost. Tip: If it runs over 1-1/2 lines, it's probably too long. Break it up.
- Use bullets to get your point across. Bullets make it easier to read and get to your point. Is it easier to read *USA Today* or *Don Quixote*?

Internet Tips

- Write your "cover letter" e-mail with short sentences that use bullets to connect you to the job requirements of the position. When you paste your résumé in the field provided on careerbuilder.com or monster.com, proof it and reconstruct the bullets and formatting that were lost, at least with spaces and dashes. Make it easier to read!

- When sending your résumé via e-mail in an ASCII format, attach (if you can) a nicely formatted one in case it does go through and the reader would like to see your creativity and preferred layout. If you do attach it, use a common program such as Microsoft Word.

- Before you e-mail your note, read it aloud as a way to proof it and send it to a friend.

- Include your e-mail address on your résumé and cover letter.

- Don't e-mail from your current employer's IP network.

- Don't circulate your work e-mail address for job search purposes.

- In the subject of your e-mail (just below the "address to" part), put something more creative than "Résumé Enclosed." Try, for example: "Résumé showing eight years in telecommunications industry" (if that is your chosen industry).

- Be careful of your spelling on the Internet. You will notice more spelling errors in e-mail exchanges than you will ever see in mailed letter exchanges.

Networking Tips

- Remember, networking is a numbers game. Once you have a network of people in place, prioritize the listing so you've separated top-priority lower-priority contacts.
- Sometimes you may have to pay for advice and information. Paying consultants or professionals or investing in Internet services is part of the job search process today, as long as it's legal and ethical.
- Know what you want from your contacts. If you don't know what you want, neither will your network of people. Specific questions will get specific answers.
- Ask for advice, not for a job. You should not contact someone and ask if that person knows of any job openings. The answer will invariably be no, especially at higher levels. You need to ask for things like industry advice and advice on geographic areas. The job insights will follow but will be almost incidental. This positioning will build value for you and make the contact person more comfortable about helping you.
- Watch your attitude and demeanor at all times. Everyone you come in contact with is a potential member of your network. Demonstrate enthusiasm and professionalism at all times.
- Get comfortable on the telephone. Good telephone communication skills are critical.
- Be well-prepared for your conversation, whether in person or over the phone. You should have a script in your mind of how to answer questions, what to ask, and what you're trying to accomplish.

- Flatter the people in your network. It's been said that the only two types of people who can be flattered are men and women. Use tact, courtesy, and flattery. Just don't appear transparent.
- If a person in your network cannot personally help, advise, or direct you, ask for referrals.
- Remember, out of sight, out of mind.
- Don't abuse the process. Networking is a two-way street. Be honest and brief and offer your contacts something in return for their time, advice, and information. This can be as simple as a lunch or an offer of your professional services in return for their cooperation.
- Show an interest in your contacts. Cavette Robert, one of the founders of the National Speakers Association, said, "People don't care how much you know until they know how much you care." Show how much you care. It will get you anywhere.
- Send thank-you notes after each networking contact.

Interviewing Tips

- Relax. The employment interview is just a meeting. Although you should not treat this meeting lightly, don't forget that the organization interviewing you is in need of your services as much as, or perhaps more than, you are of theirs.
- Be quiet and poised. Don't talk too much or too fast.
- The key to successful interviewing is building rapport. Most people spend their time preparing for interviews by memorizing canned responses to anticipated questions.

Successful interviewers spend most of their time practicing the art of building rapport through the use of powerfully effective communicating techniques.

■ Prepare a manila folder to bring to the interview. Include the following:

   Company information (annual reports, sales material, etc.)

   Extra résumés (six to 12) and your letters of reference

   15 questions you've prepared based on your research and analysis of the company

   A blank legal pad, a pen, and anything else you consider helpful (e.g., college transcripts)

■ Dress appropriately. Determine the dress code and meet it. If their dress is business casual, you still need to be dressed business professional. Practice proper grooming and hygiene.

■ Before meeting the receptionist, check your appearance. Check your hair, clothing, and general image. Test your smile.

■ Secretaries, administrative assistants, and receptionists often have a say in the hiring process. Make a strong first impression on them.

■ Your handshake should be firm and made with a wide-open hand, fingers stretched wide apart. Women should feel comfortable offering their hands for firm and friendly handshakes. A power handshake and a great smile will get you off to a great start. Just don't overdo the power handshake.

■ Eye contact is one of the most powerful forms of communication. It demonstrates confidence, trust, and power.

- During the interview lean toward the interviewer. Show enthusiasm and sincere interest.

- Take notes. You may want to refer to them later in the interview. If you're uncomfortable with this, ask permission first.

- Communicate your skills, qualifications, and credentials to the hiring manager. Describe your market value and the benefits you offer. Demonstrate how you will contribute to the bottom line. Show how you can (1) improve sales, (2) reduce costs, (3) improve productivity, and/or (4) solve organizational problems.

- Key in on specific accomplishments. Accomplishments determine hire ability.

- Let the interviewer bring up salary first. The purpose of an interview is to determine whether there is a match. Once that is determined, salary should be negotiated.

- There is no substitute for planning and preparation, practice and rehearsing—absolutely none.

- Practice interviewing techniques by using video technology. A minimum of five hours of video practice, preferably more, guarantees a stellar performance.

- Close the sale. If you find that you want the position, ask for it. Ask directly, "Is there anything that would prevent you from offering me this position now?" or "Do you have any reservations or concerns?" (if you sense that). At the very least, this should flush out any objections and give you the opportunity to turn them into positives.

- Always send a thank-you note within 24 hours of every employment meeting.

25 Salary Negotiating Tips

- Delay all discussions of salary until there is an offer on the table.
- You are in the strongest negotiating position right after the offer is made.
- Know your value. You must know how you can contribute to the organization.
- Before going into employment negotiations, you must know the average salary paid for similar positions with other organizations in your geographic area.
- Before going into employment negotiations you must know, as best you can, the salary range that the company you're interviewing with will pay or what former employees were earning.
- Remember, fringes and perks such as vacation time, flex time, health benefits, and pension plans have value. Consider the "total" salary package.
- Listen carefully and pay close attention. Your goals most likely will be different from the employer's goals. For instance, the firm's main focus might be "base salary." Yours might be "total earning potential." A win-win solution might be to negotiate a lower base salary but a higher commission or bonus structure.
- Anticipate objections and prepare effective answers to them.
- Try to understand the employer's point of view. Then plan a strategy to meet both the employer's concerns and your needs.

- Don't be afraid to negotiate because of fear of losing the offer. Most employers expect you to negotiate as long as you negotiate in a fair and reasonable manner.
- Always negotiate in a way that reflects your personality, character, and work ethic. Remain within your comfort zone.
- Play hardball only if you're willing to walk away from or lose the deal.
- What you lose in the negotiations most likely will never be recouped. Don't be careless in preparing for or conducting the negotiation.
- Be sure to get the offer and final agreement in writing.
- Never link salary to personal needs or problems. Compensation should always be linked to your value.

Part II

Perfect Management Phrases

Coaching Phrases

Coaching in business can deliver dramatic results and drive significant financial impact for an organization. Today's values-based organizations employ coaching to inspire perform-ance, develop their current and future leaders, and ensure the success of the people within. Success in anything is always about people and successful execution, in anything.

If coaching ability is important to your prospective employer, then you have to be able to effectively articulate that in a believable manner in your cover letter and in your résumé. If you just say you're a coach with nothing to back it up, the interviewer will see through it and disregard you in that way. Be specific and use examples!

Perfect Letter Phrases for Coaching

- My consulting engagements center on Executive Coaching and Leadership Development: partnering with various business executives to coach them regarding their business challenges; helping them to improve their performance and achieve their business goals. I even coached a Fortune 250 CEO regarding how his behaviors influenced his organizational culture and environment.
- As a group manager in marketing, I created and implemented "Coaches Corner Tips" to cross-pollinate sales/service scripting, improve product knowledge and soft skills, and increase sales techniques.
- While working as a project manager supporting multiple internal disciplines, we conducted 360-degree feedback sessions to gain a better understanding of our strengths and development needs. The consensus ➡

from this report identified coaching across and down as a strength for me. I have a copy of the 360 review and would be happy to bring it to our next meeting.

- I developed our group to meet and exceed company goals through coaching techniques, training, and corrective action. Our group assumed an advocate role developing and writing training courses based on development opportunities within the company.

- As the director of the call center, I supervise an average of 40 Senior Specialists, listening and coaching on an average of 20 to 25 calls daily. Providing immediate feedback is the cornerstone to effective coaching, both for great behaviors and for opportunities.

- My coaching activities focused on organizational processes, coaching/motivating staff, dealing with problem behaviors resulted in an estimated 7 percent increase in overall productivity while our staff realized a reduction of 4 percent in the same time frame.

- I am a seasoned professional with over 15 years experience leading coaching, training, documentation, and staff development in the following areas:

    Career Development

    Coaching and Performance Consulting

    Training Management/Delivery

    Distance Learning Administration

- My success in working well with those that do not report to me lies in effectively coaching through solutions with peers and other departments to reach a common goal. For example, while working on

➡

billing system changes, I had to motivate the sales organization to work with me while it was definitely outside their core competency and the behavior they were paid to exhibit.

- While at PepsiCo, I developed a program on coaching, behavioral interviewing, and retail selling.
This included:

  Designing, facilitating, and implementing intensive training lectures, seminars, and course curriculum; career excellence and personal coaching abilities.

  Classes on anger management, budgets and financial counseling, diversity in the workplace, conflict resolution, team-building, and personal coaching techniques.

Perfect Letter Phrases for Driving Performance

- Coaching a team is mandatory to high performance. My group led in calls processed and in monitored calls of excellence. We accomplished this by holding weekly one-on-one reviews and setting daily goals and expectations, and by recognizing when those goals were met or exceeded.
- Sustaining high and consistent sales for my organization made my group the highest performing within the organization. My approach to driving performance begins with people. Assessing talent and hiring great people is my cornerstone to success.
- The accounting department I managed had the highest employee satisfaction survey rating. The independent surveyor estimated that this translated to 21 percent increased productivity.

➥

- The workforce is a key value driver that is crucial to increasing shareholder value. In a study of 191 senior executives at major U.S. corporations, 92 percent believe human assets have a great effect on the ability of a company to achieve customer satisfaction, 82 percent see the impact of employees on profitability, and 72 percent see an impact on innovation and new product development.

- According to one of Fortune Magazine's "Most Desirable Companies to Work For," hiring great people is the first requirement for high performance. One great person is equal to three good people, and one good person is equal to three average people.

- Setting goals establishes a performance target for each activity, whether it is a daily sales goal, an annual one, or even the number of inquiries a call center processes. While general manager at PepsiCo, I set weekly targets of productivity for my team, and they responded by achieving a top four of 130 districts national ranking.

- Driving high performance begins with leading by example. By leading the key activities for our success myself, my team both learned how to execute and that they needed to in order to be a true part of the team.

- The "high-performance" organization owes its success to its employees. It is an indication of a learning organization that provides training in the following areas: redesign of business processes, delegation of work, teamwork, companywide communication, shared vision, and advanced technology skills. A high-performance business improves faster than its competition and sustains that rate, while satisfying all its stakeholders.

➡

- Our marketing organization identified the most critical factors to delivering the greatest possible total return to shareholders over an extended period of time—the hallmark of a high-performance business.
- Performance-driven organizations are characterized by above-average results, usually measured in financial terms, such as profit, earnings per share, revenue growth, return on invested capital, product costs, and asset utilization. Strong financial performance is an indicator of excellence elsewhere in the organization; actually, these companies outperform their competitors in customer service and satisfaction, product quality, innovation, and productivity.
- My organization led improvements in five key areas, resulting in a 53 percent increase in market value. My team's workforce management practices include:

    Implementing focused HR technology

    Opening up communications between management and employees

    Establishing a collegial, flexible workplace

    Creating a total rewards and accountability orientation

    Attaining excellence in recruitment and retention

- Teams invariably contribute significant achievements in business, charity, schools, government, communities, and the military. Overcoming barriers to performance is how groups become teams.
- Managers and others often should pay more attention to helping team leaders perform. Assuming that the team approach really is the best option, the key to ➡

getting unstuck lies in addressing the particular obstacles confronting the team with a strong performance focus. There is no incremental performance expectation beyond that provided by individual executives working within their formal areas of responsibility.

- The bottom line of performance is that organization success depends on how well the expectations of key stakeholders are met (customers, investors, employees, suppliers, and the public).
- The ABC division led performance at Goodwyn, a Fortune 75 company. Our operating redesign included the following issues:

  Benchmarking high-performance organizations, learning about high performance

  Assessing current organization strengths and weaknesses

  Creating an organization operating philosophy

  Designing the work system, including jobs, roles, and responsibilities

  Designing a performance measurement and management plan

  Creating a capability building plan: training, development experiences

  Developing a transition plan to manage the change

  Providing for continual renewal to ensure adapting to the changing environment

Managing Conflict

Conflict is not always negative. In fact, it can be healthy when effectively managed. Healthy conflict can lead to:

- Growth and innovation
- New ways of thinking
- Additional management options

There are five steps to managing conflict:

- Analyze the conflict
- Determine management strategy
- Prenegotiation
- Negotiation
- Postnegotiation

You need to position yourself as one who manages conflict well, who grows teams, keeps morale high, and drives your team or projects to "strive, stretch, and reach."

Perfect Letter Phrases for Managing Conflict

- Recruited as a contracted trainer for specialized workshop programs, I led programs including stress management, interpersonal communication skills, career management, customer service skills, conflict resolution, understanding and managing change, team building, assertiveness/self-esteem, and "Who Moved My Cheese?"
- As you mentioned the importance of bridging ideas to a successful conclusion, I acted as liaison between executives, tenants, brokers, and corporation, managing conflict and ensuring shared understanding, accountable for coordination of final agreements.

- As a project leader managing several department contributions, I resolved conflicts between departments to ensure personnel were available for flights, conducted team leader meetings, and resolved all customer problems.
- I developed and led conflict resolution programs in schools linking leadership program with life skills awareness within a Baldridge in Education framework.
- I created an annual culture survey and consulted with management teams on potential suggestions to enhance/improve culture. This resulted in:

  My organization was responsible for driving change and managing new staffing models utilizing the "workout" change model by leading a team of 30 cross functional managers:

  - Facilitated several conflict resolution sessions between operations and functional groups
  - Facilitated new manager assimilation sessions
  - Facilitated change management work-out sessions

- Managing conflict successfully has more to do with acting as a coach, not a cop.
- My past successes demonstrate strengths in managing diverse job processes, building and maintaining relationships throughout an organization, motivating staff and colleagues, assessing and developing high potential talent, and managing corporate objectives through major change.
- I attended the following classes in the effort to hone my coaching and interpersonal management skills:

➡

Managing Conflict: AT&T School of Business, Course MS6431, completed

Managing People and Performance: AT&T School of Business, Course MD7601, completed October 1993

Certifications: Numerous technical and managerial courses: Managing People and Performance, Managing Conflict, Communications Workshop, Leadership for the Future, Achieving Communication Effectiveness, and Labor Relations (AT&T School of Business & Technology)

- Conflict can be constructive, but if left to "work itself out," the outcomes are seldom acceptable to all parties. Not only will mismanaged conflict disrupt the best of plans, it also dissipates energy and distracts from your goals.
- A key requirement of any great internal success coach prepares training materials and leads workshops on Stress Management, Understanding and Managing Change (incorporating "Who Moved My Cheese?" materials), Career Development and Advancement.
- In 2006, I was selected local facilitator for the nationwide training broadcasts, Coaching Skills for Managers, Planning and Organizing, Oral Communications and Listening Skills, Training Aids, and Training Technology Update. I am a certified facilitator for group feedback sessions for managerial and support staff who completed the "Performance Development System's" training assessment instrument.

High Employee Satisfaction

High employee satisfaction is essential in recruiting and hiring a quality workforce. Tracking the attitudes and opinions of employees can identify problem areas and solutions related to management and leadership, corporate policy, recruitment, benefits, diversity, training, and professional development. A comprehensive employee satisfaction study can be the key to a more motivated and loyal workforce.

Good managers and good companies realize a happy employee is a productive employee. Poor managers might lead by intimidation, fear, or be too far the other way and appear lackadaisical. A good sports coach knows that to squeeze out that extra level of performance, the athlete must be motivated and driven.

Driven and motivated employees will be more creative and work harder to solve problems because they care about their careers and about the company or organization with whom they work.

For your part in this, you want to be the manager or employee who creates this drive for excellence, who is able to get the team to perform high by being highly satisfied. With your cover letters, if this is an important trait of the hiring manager, you definitely want to address it in a letter or e-mail.

Consider the following phrases for articulating that you have and can create high employee satisfaction.

Perfect Letter Phrases Demonstrating High Employee Satisfaction

- I organized and participated as a lead in task forces set up by management to improve employee satisfaction in 2003, and the results showed a much better rating in 2004.

- Facilitating employee growth through a culture of openness, continuous feedback, and a practice of prompt decision making (most employee concerns addressed within one working day) has made CPG a "Top Company to Work For," according to *Fortune* magazine's 2005 annual review.
- We started employee involvement groups to improve morale and safety, which resulted in one recorded and no loss-time injuries in past year. Our CEO states that morale has never been higher. Employee turnover decreased from 35 to 5 percent.
- As general manager I implemented a performance management process, which created a strong overachieving team with high employee satisfaction and a less than 5 percent turnover rate.
- In 2006, I won the Award of Excellence in recognition of exceptional employee relations for six consecutive years, as voted on by management. This exemplifies the important characteristics of high integrity, loyalty, and dedication.
- Increased productivity 25 percent overall with reduced staff turnover and high employee satisfaction by creating a positive, teamwork environment, setting goals and sharing the vision.
- We consistently achieved high employee satisfaction, resulting in minimal employee attrition numbers. We also maintained a 90 percent or better rate of retention for the senior seasonal staff team, and zero percent turnover for full-time staff for two consecutive years.

➡

- As a Human Resources director, I have always resolved employee/employer issues fairly and effectively, which contributed to high employee satisfaction.
- Our call center productivity improved at least 40 percent and achieved a high employee satisfaction rating as evidenced by an independent study by planning, managing, and monitoring personnel, labor relations, and training.
- The HR organization I led managed a $1 million project that increased office morale, customer service, and diversity ratings, according to T.D. Finley Rating Survey, by 50 percent.
- In 2004 we introduced employee financial/award incentives that improve productivity and reduce absenteeism, resulting in a 15 percent increase in gross profits. That year we achieved the highest percentage of employee advancement in the organization.
- In order to improve employee loyalty and satisfaction, we worked with management to create a program offering free, in-house, leading industry certifications. This program offered employees optional classes in the evenings within our shop for courses leading to certifications such as MCSE and CNE. There were visible improvements with employee satisfaction, and we had a less than 2 percent turnover during the program's two years.
- I have always provided face-to-face contact needed to resolve sensitive employee issues, including terminations, violence in the workplace issues, harassment/discrimination investigations, and labor relations issues. I even partnered with Senior/

➡

Executive Business Leaders to deploy business initiatives and to improve employee satisfaction.

- As the corporate culture champion, I am responsible for department and centerwide employee satisfaction results. Achieved improvement in employee satisfaction through implementation of employee-focused initiatives.

Part III

Individual Performance Phrases

Cost Reduction

It's no coincidence that the most effective cost cutters are companies like Wal-Mart Stores Inc. or Dell Inc., which use technology to keep processes such as inventory management at the cutting edge. Cost reduction in general is a big part of business. It has always had its place, but more since the economic climate softened in 2000. Events since then have compounded the economic instability, and countless companies have made drastic measures to reduce costs to remain viable.

In the telecom industry in particular, cost reduction, not limited to but impacted by workforce reduction, has been paramount for survival.

Here is what you need to be aware of: Cost reduction always has value. You need to position the cost reduction measures in your discipline in association with improved performance of some kind, not just eliminating a workforce or particular product or function. Associate reduction of costs with improved performance and then you'll really have something to talk about.

The phrases below are to be used as a template for articulating a more substantive description of how you drove reduction in costs. You won't be able use all these exact phrases because some are specific to the given candidate's accomplishments. Use them as a guideline to be more specific rather than general. Don't be vague!

Perfect Letter Phrases for Cost Reduction

- As the call center director, I reduced costs by redesigning front and back office call center processes for a 100

➡

MM-plus annual inbound operations, which led to a cost reduction of 18 percent per member in FY06.

- I took on an extracurricular project to rewrite and implement a new safety handbook resulting in an immediate 25 percent reduction in workers compensation claims.
- My finance organization led to the reduction in direct labor cost by $2.5 million on an annual budget of $12 million. We even drove employee incentive programs, which cost-reduced operation by $1 million.
- My team led a successful turnaround from a $1.5 million loss to $.5 million profit in one year; reduced breakeven cost by more than 30 percent, and delivered a 50 percent quality improvement. I led the development of a growth plan for equity investment and refinancing, and implemented key operational changes that drove profitability improvements. We exceeded cost reduction goals by more than 245 percent, delivering over $100,000 in savings in the first year.
  [*Note: try to be specific when describing so your message is not vague and does not appear fake or made up. Even this could be more specific.*]
- The transitional team I lead developed the business case for an inbound telemarketing acquisition vehicle, leading to a significant reduction in acquisition costs (14 percent) and to an incremental 2 million annual registrations.
- As plant manager, I supervised the printing plant production and performed efficiency studies of equipment and operations that resulted in waste reduction from 8 to 3.5 percent, and production increases of 15 percent.

➡

Customer complaints reduced to zero.

- I led cost reduction and efficiency activities during revenue downturn, improving the bottom line 5 percent despite 13 percent revenue reduction.
- I was assigned as project manager for the PRI, working with "Global Shared Services," to reduce total cost of ownership of digital output devices (printers-copiers-faxes), establishing processes, standards, and enabling Web access and usage monitoring for cost containment and reduction of nonbusiness activities by minimizing unauthorized use. A 10 to 15 percent cost reduction was projected after a complete cost/benefit analysis and equipment inventory was completed.
- We accomplished the reduction of inventory by 24 percent, utilizing MRP [Management Resource Planning], JIT [Just in Time], and Value Managed Partnerships with suppliers.
- I created the first Corporate Inventory Reduction Program, achieving 15 percent reduction in inventories, reducing carrying costs and interest charges.
- My group implemented cost containment strategies for medical and workmen's compensation programs.
- As chief negotiator, I lead in negotiations with the UAW and URW. Major achievements in latest UAW contract (6-03) include COLA savings of $1 million and 30 percent reduction in medical absenteeism, saving $2 million.
- While balancing the requirements to have a cost effective marketing and distribution system with a progressive organization capable of generating explosive growth, I identified cost containment and restructuring opportunities that led to a total 75

➡

basis point decrease in sales acquisition cost, a 32 percent reduction while increasing sales $2.3 billion, almost a 50 percent increase. Cost reductions have allowed for additional promotional opportunities, increased price competitiveness, and a self-financed expansion into new distribution channels.

- My leadership over an executive team was responsible for the reduction of over $65 million in annual expenses prior to the purchase of Ameritech by SBC.

Negotiation

Negotiation skills are an important part of business and life. You negotiate every day without even knowing. I negotiate every morning with my wife or son and don't even notice, losing too many to my son, which encroaches on time management, another section!

The strength of your agreements, understandings, and relationships can mean the difference between success and failure. Weak agreements with companies and individuals always break down. They bring nagging dissatisfaction and aggravation into your business and personal lives. Strong agreements help you reach and exceed your own objectives, and leave the other party gaining more satisfaction at the same time.

Negotiating is important for everyone, but particularly for those who work in sales, purchasing, legal, or for any senior level manager.

When you do craft a message around your negotiating skills, be specific. Just saying you have excellent negotiating skills says nothing. You need to offer some specifics to lend credibility.

Perfect Letter Phrases for Negotiating

- Managing $200 million in government contracts and $600 million in proposal efforts required skillful negotiating skills. I led full-life-cycle negotiation and administration of federal government solicitations and contracts for AT&T's government service offerings.
- As a client executive, I negotiated enterprise and nonenterprise agreements with major software and

consulting services suppliers that resulted in substantial cost savings, cost avoidance, and risk mitigation.

- With limited available negotiation leverage, my team renegotiated software support agreements that resulted in dramatic decreases in total costs of ownership for software support and maintenance agreements. In 2006, I attended the Karrass Effective Negotiating Techniques seminar.

- Having led negotiations in both vertical and horizontal environments, I am adept in developing alternative language and resolving disagreements during negotiations with customers, partners, and vendors in international, commercial, and government markets.

- A financial pricing director must be an accomplished contract negotiator and manager, with international work-location experience, and over 10 successful years developing, drafting, negotiating, and managing sales and other customer-related contracts. Typical contracts include: distribution, reseller, OEM, and government.

- In 2004, I negotiated all-time charter business with major oil companies and traders. This included supervising all spot charter negotiations in conjunction with operations, legal, engineering, insurance, financial, and personnel departments. My group negotiated eight overseas new building construction contracts in excess of $400 million.

- I am a professionally certified and highly experienced sourcing, contracts, and procurement manager with diverse and comprehensive domestic and international procurement, strategic sourcing, contract, project management, logistics management, subcontract management, supplier management, and negotiations experience.

- As the senior contract administrator at Masco, the fifth largest company in Miami, I was responsible for drafting, reviewing, negotiating, and administering contracts relating to commercial aviation; researching federal, state, and international laws and regulations; and making recommendations to senior management on creating compliant company procedures and contractual terms.
- From 1999 to 2004, I was the number three national accounts manager at IBM, servicing existing accounts and developing new accounts, making presentations and negotiating agreements, and closing sales. As a top national accounts manager, negotiating agreements that would breed mutual satisfaction was my strongest suit. In fact, I once negotiated an $18-MM agreement with a Wachovia VP over a dinner napkin to close our region's largest sale in 2003.
- As a contract specialist for P&G, I drafted and managed RFPs, RFIs, and RFQs, even working with Legal to create our first boilerplate.
- As the head of legal counsel, I am the lead negotiator for corporate contracts, statements of work, amendments for outsourcing of IT and Finance and Accounting services, and acquisition of information technology and professional services.
- I participated on the negotiating team on the largest alliance in company history: Chrysler strategic alliance ($800-MM investment in company as part of overall agreement).

    Reviewed over 200 proposals and worked on 10 teams focused on specific deals (partnerships, strategic equity investments, acquisition, etc.). ➡

Represented Chrysler corporate development as an advisor to business units and Internet team—targeting, reviewing, negotiating, performing due diligence on projects related to the Internet, devices, applications, and new partnerships and technologies.

Managed transaction and project pipeline process as well as the unsolicited proposal evaluation process based on Chrysler's strategic priorities for all business units and business development activities.

Oral Presentations

Oral communication skills are critical to the success of individuals and their organizations. This is equally true whether you are communicating one-to-one or one-to-250. A good presentation has the power to deliver your message and the emotional force to move your audience to new ways of thinking and/or behaving.

Delivering oral presentations or having excellent oral presentation skills is important to any position, but perhaps more vital to those in training, sales, marketing, consulting, and to senior management in general. In almost every letter I read, the candidate writes "excellent oral [or presentation] skills." Fine. So what? Everything you write should answer the question, "So what?"

Consider modeling your phrases the way the following more specific phrases are written.

Perfect Letter Phrases for Oral Presentations

- As a trainer for ACR, I develop and deliver presentations that excite and inform. Excellence in training skills include developing and delivering training curriculum, including the presentations and workbooks.
- My experience as an engaging speaker and seminar leader, sales presenter, and technical management liaison has made me the most skilled motivator in the organization. I have a natural ability to work with others, influence C-level decision making, and promote company products and services to a wide range of targeted prospects, alliance partners, and vendor leaders.

➡

- I have presented to more than 30 Fortune 500 CXOs in the effort to practice consultative sales techniques, uncovering the needs of the client, and developing valuable solutions.
- I have effectively promoted company products through oral presentations in a variety of venues, including trade shows and conferences, to create exciting "buzz." I am regularly requested to speak at industry trade conferences [*you might be more specific here*] and global billing and trade shows.
- I have delivered over a thousand lectures, primarily for Ford Motor Company, Fidelity, and Anderson Consulting, and am recognized by *Marketing and Sales* magazine as one of the top 10 speakers in the United States. In 1999, I was recognized by the WTC in Dallas as "America's number one motivational technology speaker."
- In 2005, I wrote the keynote speech for a motivational speaker. I doubled the original content through extensive research and interviews, and made countless revisions to make the tone and texture of the language sound consistent with the speaker's personal style. The presentation received excellent audience feedback and a repeat invitation from the speaker for the 2006 CTIA show.
- As a marketing and motivational speaker, I participated in training classes through the delivery of entertaining and informative lectures to middle and high school students. Topics include those that encourage and support self-confidence, social skills, etc. The audience number ranged from 30 to 300 plus.
- Communication includes effective speaking and writing skills. As an experienced public speaker: I conducted

➥

training seminars for candidates, volunteers, and party activists; served as a liaison between different personality types; am comfortable and effective communicating with both superiors and staff.

- You mentioned team building is critical to success in this position. At my current employer, I am an organizational leader, trainer, and educator recognized for my ability to merge dissimilar people into cohesive teams with common focus.

Organizational Skills

I interviewed a candidate named Steve some time ago and hired him based on his ability to manage multiple projects simultaneously. His résumé listed: "Excellent organizational skills." Then I worked with him, and within 90 days it proved to be blatantly untrue. Steve could not plan or manage multiple projects or issues simultaneously. Sometimes I wondered how I missed it during the interview. I was faked out. I now discount that phrase "excellent organizational skills" as a hiring manager unless it is supported.

That's the key—to support the skill with some backup, so it seems credible, and not with cover letter fluff. Consider the following phrases and how they are supported. Notice that the actual phrase "organizational skills" is not always present; it is implied, which is perhaps even more powerful.

Perfect Letter Phrases Demonstrating Organizational Skills

- My 15 years experience in managing multiple projects simultaneously, including the ability to work under pressure, meet tight deadlines, and utilize problem-solving skills to ensure projects met stated goals and objectives, is a very good fit for your operations management position.
- My success lies in leading revenue generation programs with particular skill in managing multiple projects simultaneously from concept to completion.
- I consistently bring projects to a successful finish on time and on budget by successfully managing multiple projects simultaneously and effectively managing my time.

- In 2005, I was promoted to lead the Project Management Team. I managed all aspects of the division's business and systems projects by preparing and managing project plans, scheduling and facilitating status meetings, and evaluating and analyzing cost-benefit relationships.
- As a principle at Arrow Consulting, project management for marketing programs is a cornerstone of successful engagements and in building a client base. I am experienced in all areas of targeted marketing, retail management, and ad production and printing, and at managing multiple projects simultaneously.
- My organization led a strategic marketing plan for the company, researched and evaluated new safety software, provided detailed case research and accident reconstruction support for ongoing litigation, and published press releases, all of which contributed to a successful IPO in 2006.
- Working with cross-functional teams, I achieve win-win outcomes through strong organizational skills with an acute attention to detail, ability to manage multiple projects simultaneously, and excellent analytical, follow-through, and decision-making skills.
- As managing account executive, I am responsible for marketing, coordinating, and managing vendor services for large corporate accounts. My group represented multiple regional vendor services, specializing in worker's compensation, auto, medical malpractice, and disability insurance, requiring excellent organizational skills and project planning.
- I was recruited to provide risk, logistics, inventory, facility and warehouse operations management, including

➥

personnel supervision, for a leading remanufacturer of consumer electronic products. This position requires excellent organizational skills in order to manage all functional areas properly. Responsibilities included coordinating international logistics between multiple manufacturing and refurbishment centers, and establishing and managing the reverse logistics department, handling over 15,000 units per year.

- At Cisco Systems, I managed the partner program support, including the production and distribution of Electronic Partner Packages, multiple collateral projects (data sheets and Division Overview brochure), trade show collateral, and signage requirements.

- A successful coordinator effectively manages integrated marketing programs with limited resources from development and implementation to program reporting and analysis. I am experienced at consulting with teams to understand their needs, uncovering opportunities, and recommending creative ideas and solutions.
I also have proven skills in organizing, prioritizing, and managing multiple projects simultaneously on time and budget.

- My sales support organization interfaced with three regional sales centers and with field marketing to develop projects targeting installed customers to increase customer loyalty. Under my leadership we developed and managed integrated marcom projects from concept to completion.

- I managed the creative development of sales literature, including product software specification sheets, brochures, reference guides, and case studies. Success

➡

lay in ensuring completion of projects on time and within budget guidelines. I worked with various agencies regarding copywriting, design, and print production, managing multiple projects simultaneously.

- I was recruited to develop a communication strategy to ensure that group goals were being tracked and that they met project deadlines. While I was the managing partner, I developed streamlined project tracking processes that resulted in acquisitions of over $53 million, while managing multiple projects simultaneously with outside vendors.

- The plant for which I was responsible increased production efficiency by an average of 14 percent annually for three years. I accomplished this by managing multiple projects simultaneously, including client relations, schedules, and deadlines.

Problem Solving

A manager's primary function is to solve problems. A manager's understanding of the problem-solving style he or she most often uses is an essential early step to becoming a more effective and creative problem solver.

Managers tend to deal with problems in one of three ways:

1. **Avoid them.** Refuse to recognize that a problem exists. Not quite the strongest managers, but I have had the pleasure of knowing some of these folks. Some people just don't understand most problems do not self-correct.

2. **Solve them as necessary.** Deal with the urgent. Better, but still not senior management material.

3. **Seek them out.** Anticipate, to avoid the problems becoming urgent. You want to be here! This is where you need to position yourself and represent your skills on your résumé and during the interview.

Perfect Letter Phrases for Problem Solving

- I have always been a creative problem solver. My experience moving beyond limiting questions and nurturing problem-solving ideas through each of four phases of creative problem solving has resulted in a very solid foundation.

- As a hospital administrator, success has included strategic thinking and 10 years of solving design, communication, and process problems.

- Having been promoted to account management with Chiat-Day, a leading advertising firm, I managed all

➡

print and presentation projects, exceeding a 95 percent on-time rate. I handled project tracking, system/file management, estimating, budget/billing, vendor billing, and liaisons with all clients.

- A veteran production manager, I am experienced with quality assurance, problem solving, streamlining processes, and optimizing production work flow. Succeeding in my position requires extensive experience in project management, creating intuitive business collateral, Internet promotion, and developing proactive marketing strategies.
- My strength is a problem-solving ability: analyzing the symptoms, identifying what is wrong, and finding the solution.
- At Ford Motor, I implemented the following structured programs and methods into the engineering department: Advanced Quality Planning, Dimensional Control Plan Plus, Failure Mode and Effects Analysis, Design of Experiments, Quality Operating System, 8-D Problem Administration, and Planning & Problem Solving.
- A core strength of mine is overseeing multiple tasks with varying priorities, working with many departments within an organization to ensure smooth operation, identifying areas of improvement, as well as researching, developing, and implementing improved procedures. An example includes … [*Use one relevant to the target company's business.*]
- My vice president has always recognized my ability in problem solving, with a strong background in methods and time studies for setting production standards. This is particularly relevant in assessing and resolving

➡

employee conflicts and organizational problems, allowing for increased productivity.

- I developed strategic relationships with various department heads and suppliers, which significantly improved communication and problem resolution capabilities within the organization.
- I have applied strong interpersonal and communication skills in working with a wide range of personnel at all levels to gain valuable insight, avoid potential problems, and facilitate the timely completion of projects.
- As a claims manager, I successfully implemented customer deductions programs, which identified problem areas within the corporation and reported results. I then made recommendations to senior management on a daily basis in written review summaries.

Time Management

Time management is a vital skill for a successful person, in any discipline. No question. So many people think they have it and so few do. I had a vice president several years ago who used to say, "Give me someone smart, passionate, and who knows how to use their time, and we can give them the experience." Same with time management for me. It's vital to success. If you can convey that you effectively manage multiple projects simultaneously, you will be much more valuable to your prospective employer. Then call me because I want you working with me!

Don't let anyone steal your time. It is priceless and should be guarded with care. Benjamin Franklin once said, "Dost thou love life? Then do not squander time, for that is the stuff life is made of." More recently, Henry Kissinger, former Secretary of State said, "There cannot be a crisis next week. My schedule is already full." Needless to say, the most valuable commodity in the world is time. It is easily wasted and can never be replaced; therefore, time management is essential.

Consider the following phrases, employed to convince employers that these candidates use their time effectively.

Perfect Letter Phrases for Time Management

- While a district manager with Lane Bryant, sales and time management skills were required for success:

  Conducted training needs assessments for 23 stores to determine training shortfalls and needs.

  Attended several sales and time management courses (i.e., Covey, Franklin, Career Path),

  ➡

> Developed and conducted specific training courses that addressed the needs of our business.
>
> Provided consultation services in time management training to four other peer district managers.

- Excelling as a plant manager in a large-scale production environment requires excellent time management skills and the ability to meet deadlines and work under pressure. My team led productivity targets by leading the floor, training the staff, and anticipating problems before they occurred.
- [Hiring manager], you mentioned being successful in this role requires strong time management skills. While general manager for Aramark, my success required finding out how much time is worth, concentrating on the right things, deciding work priorities, planning to solve a problem, tackling the right tasks first through prioritized "to do" lists, and executing the plan timely.
- As advertising account manager I utilized extensive project coordination, prioritization, and details/time management techniques to keep all schedules on track and time sensitive projects on time and on budget.
- I am certified in time management through the Franklin Covey Education series.
- At SE Toyota, I sponsored an 80:20 program, which argues that typically 80 percent of unfocused effort generates only 20 percent of results. The remaining 80 percent of results are achieved with only 20 percent of the effort. This led to a new initiative to improve time management skills of 670-plus employees. The company estimates we improved productivity

➡️

by 17 percent the first year, very high by industry standards.

- I assisted in the implementation of SAP R/3 as the time management deployment lead, and directed the implementation of the time management module at each factory site. I also assumed the lead site payroll and HR personnel with data mapping and conversion, and instructed site power users and end users in time management training classes.
- Having been promoted to senior project manager, I demonstrated how to prioritize tasks, organize and coordinate activities, manage time, set and achieve goals, meet deadlines, develop relationships, and establish procedures.
- I assisted the production coordinator by leading the floor, training the staff, and pulling statistics. Skills used include: time management, ability to meet strict deadlines, and the ability to work under pressure.
- Your [position] requires an organized, detail-oriented, and self-motivated professional with excellent time management, prioritization, and multiple task/project coordination skills. I have demonstrated that in my past two positions, and my ability to manage time effectively was the main reason I earned an internal promotion.
- My current role as project manager enabled me to become certified in an active listening course, Decker Communication Course, and Franklin Time Management.
- Time management to me is the ability to manage multiple assignments and maintain quality of service under fast-paced conditions.
- I trained the clients' project team and determined the global template functionality for the global project

➡

team in the U.S. Duties included project plan preparation, progress reporting, training of local project team, determining local requirements, identification and specification of system interfaces, final configuration of the system, and system and acceptance testing. Modules configured and implemented were PA, PD, Training and Events, Recruitment, and Time Management.

- Effective time management required me to list out tasks, prioritize them, and map out execution of them all. I do not procrastinate, but rather use my time wisely, plan exceptionally, and employ the Covey planning system.

Written Skills

Having written a dozen books on topics like this book, I am biased concerning the importance of writing in business. I majored in accounting and never thought about the importance of writing early in my career. In fact, pride had more to do with my attention to detail in writing than anything: I never wanted to be caught with a typo or obvious incorrect grammar and have the reader think I was less professional or not queued to be promoted.

Good writing skills are an absolute reflection on your professional skills. Much of it is in proofreading and some attention to detail. I'll tell you this: When you write poorly, people think less of you professionally.

Demonstrating excellent writing skills begins with writing letters and e-mails. What follows are some phrases to consider to prove that you do in fact have excellent writing skills. Note how detailed and specific some of the descriptions are written. As a hiring manager, I would not doubt the writing skills of candidates like these.

Perfect Letter Phrases for Writing Skills

- In preparation for the 2006 CES Show, I wrote preview briefs for two clients that were used at industry seminars.
- As a product manager, I built briefing books for clients utilizing information obtained from various sources.
- My accomplishments include validating other consultants' plans, thoughts, and presentations for their clients. I provide consulting, business plan and market plan assistance, preparation for multiple presentations, marketing brochures, and mailing programs for a diversity of companies.

➡

- I worked with creative directors and training managers to develop, implement, create, and design staff instruction manuals, newsletters, Web pages, policy and procedure manuals, and announcements to publicize various training programs using Excel, PowerPoint, Word, and Lotus Notes.
- I led the layout, design, and production of printed materials, including newsletters, brochures, slides, graphs, and other visual PowerPoint presentation materials. I created Excel/Access spreadsheets, database, word processing, and graphics computer software programs.
- My support role requires being highly resourceful, possessing strong merchandising and visual presentation skills, and strong attention to detail. I also have a keen sense of color, balance, and scale. Past accomplishments include drafting the sales boilerplate, presentations, and statement of work outlines.
- As a client manager, I led the client communications, product branding, product rollouts (creative and tactical implementation), communication templates, proposal style guides, process documentation, and ad campaign development.
- A successful marketing communications copywriter writes copy for marketing pieces, including but not limited to product sheets, press releases, brochures and flyers, ad copy, board reports, and client communications, which I have done with much success for PepsiCo for the past two years.
- Currently I am senior technical writer under contract to Sprint. There, I developed the Sprint Proposal Library, which included writing and editing proposal materials,

proposal boilerplate, forms, templates, technical manuals, technical requirements, and design reports.

- I served as Web editor responsible for writing and maintaining content, including service offering descriptions, value propositions, FAQs, news items, and seed content for online community. Key accomplishments include:

    Manage content administration for Web site, including updates, revisions, and posting of new material (ATG/Interwoven content management system).

    Redevelopment of Web sites, including page design, site structure, and navigation.

    Researched, developed, and wrote Web-based, interactive business training (included instructional story and material); quizzes and tutoring; expert interviews and audio; glossary and FAQs; conceptualized and worked with tech staff to develop multimedia component that reinforced instructional material.

    Developed informational resource articles on work/life issues; identified new areas and ideas for development, including resources, tools, and potential alliance partners.

Part IV

Job-Search-Related Phrases

Follow-Up Letters

I interviewed a regional manager candidate about a year ago and was on the fence: He was amply qualified—maybe too qualified—and I questioned his desire and commitment. I decided to wait it out and see what he did following the interview. I never heard from him, and moved forward with another candidate.

In many cases, the difference between success and failure is follow-up. Most people send out a résumé and expect that someone will call. It is not a strategy that breeds accomplishment. The mission is to produce actions—interviews and meetings. Follow-up letters are tools to inspire such action when original tactics fall short of expectation.

Perfect Phrases for Follow-Up Letters

- After reviewing my notes from our conversation, it is evident that you require a dynamic person who will not only generate sales revenue, but also play an integral part in maintaining International's position as a "leading edge" supplier of world-class packaging equipment. In my present role, I do this every day.

- After reviewing my résumé, perhaps you may think that I am overqualified and my compensation exceeds the level of pay anticipated for this particular position. To put your concerns to rest, the opportunity to join your group is an opportunity I do not want to pass by. Although my compensation has averaged $115,000, my salary requirements are flexible, considering future opportunities for growth within the organization. I would welcome a personal interview to further discuss the search and

➡

am confident that the outcome would be beneficial to future KPMG business results. I appreciate you passing this information along.

- Again, thank you for meeting with me and affording an opportunity to discuss the position with you and Ms. Jennings. If I can answer any further questions, please feel free to contact me at the telephone number listed above. I look forward to speaking with you soon.

- I am confident that my strengths will help you to create a greater customer focus, which will in turn boost earnings and raise morale. Could we speak soon about my possible contributions to Smyth Insurance? Thank you for your time; I eagerly await the opportunity to meet with you in person.

- Our meeting at the end of the day revealed that my technical capabilities could fit into a number of areas at Dartwalsh. My conversation with Mike Tarmew concerning laser technology and high-speed through-put leads me to believe that this is an area where you may have a need I can fill. However, I remain open to exploring a variety of opportunities to find the best match. I will call you next Friday morning to set up another meeting.

- I am writing to follow up on the letter and résumé I sent you on February 16 last year. You were recruiting for a product manager with experience in voice and data integration and experience selling in the Fortune 250 arena. I am a product manager with IBM with four years of product sales experience and have presented to over 30 CXOs from the Fortune 250.

- I want to thank you for your candor in explaining why you did not choose me for the position I interviewed

➡

for two years ago. I understand that you wanted someone with more than my one year of experience in health care administration. I now have three years of experience.

- Nearly a year ago you and I met to discuss an opening in your sales department. We were in the process of setting up a second meeting when I called to let you know that I had accepted a position at Haverty's.

- May I ask whether you are still recruiting for your accounting office, for which I applied on January 30?

- I know you have been away on business, but I am wondering if you received my letter of January 7. I sent you a brief business plan outlining what I would do if given the opportunity to lead the new marketing initiative we discussed.

- In response to your district manager posting of August 18, I forwarded my résumé, two references, and a cover letter. Since I have received no response, I am wondering if my materials failed to reach you. My background is a very close fit with the position requirements described.

- As a follow-up to our telephone conversation of May 16, here is an updated copy of my résumé.

- During our telephone conversation yesterday afternoon you offered to forward my résumé to your Springfield office. Here is an updated copy that I would appreciate you sending. Thank you very much for your help.

Internal Job Search

Pursuing job opportunities internally is much different than pursuing them externally. The biggest difference is spin and positioning. While you should always be truthful when representing your qualifications externally, your spin is severely limited, communicating internally versus externally.

Externally, no one really knows if you were the nerve center behind Apple's resurgence with the iPod or not. However, if you work for Apple, well, your qualifications are much more widely known and can be validated.

There are pluses and minuses to each form of communication. With an internal communication, you need to leverage two things: relationships and accomplishments. Internal sponsorship is critical to moving around internally or particularly in getting promoted internally. I recall my first director position, which I took several years ago. When I interviewed with the vice president, he expressed two potential concerns before bringing me on.

Once I understood them, I rallied all my supporters from within the organization and scripted them with key messages to offset his concerns. Some were written in e-mail form and some were voice mail. The point is to leverage relationships.

Below are some great introductory phrases for internal letters, usually e-mails.

Perfect Phrases for Internal Job Search

- Mr. Levin, Lisa Pearman suggested I contact you about the new senior engineering manager position in your group. I have worked for Lisa for two years and she speaks very highly of you and encouraged me to

➡

contact you, thinking it would be a great mutual fit.

- As you know, I have worked with you for two years as Marketing Manager of P&G's soap division. As we discussed yesterday, I am ready to move on to the Group Manager position in the family products group. As my director, you have been able to observe that contribution firsthand. But I felt it would be a good idea to take inventory of my achievements.

- I am writing to formally express interest in being considered as a candidate for the Field Service Revenue Administration Manager. I have attached an up-to-date copy of my résumé as well as a memo detailing salient project accomplishments over the past 18 months. I present the following highlights …

- As a seasoned sales manager with Wagner and Poles (four years as Sales Manager, seven years total), I am armed with extensive expertise in developing new business, turning around sluggish sales, and significantly impacting growth and profits. I believe I am well qualified for the position of National Key Account Manager within our organization, and have enclosed a résumé outlining my highlights and contributions with regard to Wagner and Poles.

Networking

Networking is widely recognized as the most effective technique in securing employment opportunities. Networking is the process of engaging your network of family, friends, and associates to help you identify and obtain the job you desire. I think of networking as connecting dots, creating your own six degrees of separation.

The networking cover letter is a letter communicating to your network of contacts that you are seeking advice and information, not a job as the short-term objective. The letter clearly defines your skills, what types of opportunities you are seeking, and specific organizations you'd like to work for. It is still true, like it or not, that it is not so much *what* you know that counts but *who* you know.

An effectively written networking letter will help you (1) to take full advantage of your network of contacts or (2) to begin developing/improve a network to expand your influence.

Below are some terrific phrases designed to help you craft a great networking letter that will help you reach the decision makers in the industries and companies you target.

Perfect Phrases for Networking Letters

- Dave Tinker from Cellcorp suggested I contact you. He said that you "know more about the network router business than anyone this side of the Mason-Dixon line." I knew you would be someone I had to meet. Though I am employed with Bell Atlantic, I have decided to make a career move toward a more entrepreneurial upstart operation. I am not writing you for a position, but rather wanted to get some industry advice from you …

➡

- I don't know if you will remember, but we met when your firm was doing some auditing work for Texas Oil. I was performing some legal work, as I am an attorney specializing in environmental law. I was very impressed with you and your team, and have a small favor to ask. I have been with my firm for some time and am interested in leaving in favor of a smaller firm. You seemed to know a lot about the industry as well as who's who in Dallas, and I'd like to ask your advice on the business climate here.

- Thanks for speaking with me on the phone earlier. I agree that there probably isn't a good match between your current positions and me to fill. However, you did mention that based on our phone interview you thought my credentials were strong, and it got me thinking. Would you mind if we still met? I am new to the New York area, as my husband was just transferred, and it looks like we'll be here for quite a while. You seemed to be fairly well connected and in the know as to what's going on here. I would love to meet just to get your advice on which firms I might avoid, which ones might be good, and what the overall climate is like in New York.

- May I ask your advice and assistance? As you know, for the last eight years I've been continuously challenged with new marketing assignments for PepsiCo and I've delivered impressive sales and profit gains for all of the brands I've managed. Grace, since you know my abilities and potential to contribute, would you take a moment to think about people I can contact at large manufacturing/consumer goods businesses in the Cincinnati area? I'm confident that I can bring to my next employer the same strong results I delivered for PepsiCo ... In addition to any contacts you can suggest, I would greatly appreciate your insight with regard to the Cincinnati job market. To assist you in evaluating appropriate contacts and suggestions, I have enclosed a ...

- I need your advice. You are a friend who has developed a fast track career, one of the company's youngest directors. I am at a career crossroads and would like to get your opinion of what you think of my current position versus a new opportunity I am considering. I'd prefer to speak to you directly about this rather than go into detail in a letter. Could we get together sometime next week to discuss my situation? I'll give you a call in the next few days to set a time. Thank you for your time.

Reference Letters

A reference letter is delivered under the writer's signature, but they will likely want your help for two reasons:

First, it takes a lot of time to sit down and create a letter like this.

Second, give them some idea of how to spin the tone and subject. Give them some information about the position or company and help them position you in the most effective light. After they write the letter, make sure you get a copy, even if they send it directly to the employer/recruiter.

In the end, however, it is recommended that you write the *outline* for the reference letter yourself. Superstars don't write the ads we see on television. The advertising agencies and marketing departments do. You are your own marketing department unless you also hire marketing professionals.

Perfect Phrases for Reference Letters

- We have had the pleasure of associating with [you, the candidate] over the past seven years with MCI and Alcalon Systems. In my 30-plus years in the business, all with Xerox, I have never met a more professional, talented, or personable warehouse manager.
- [Your name] is a strong and formidable negotiator. He always has the best interest of his company at heart. He is fair and always looks for a win-win solution to any negotiation.
- [Your name] is a loyal and dedicated professional who will enhance any company. His value, when measured against his peers, is truly head and shoulders above the rest. Proctor and Gamble will be pleased to provide

➡

you with any additional information you need. Contact me at the above address, and I will quickly respond to your inquiries.

- Any company fortunate to have [you, the candidate] as marketing manager has a true advantage in today's highly competitive economic climate. UOS has benefited from [your] expertise in management, employee, and customer relations for 12 years. [Your] independent management style allowed UOS to grow 480 percent over a 12-year period, and [you] kept his warehouse operations one step ahead of the rest of the competition.

- We all but begged [your name] to relocate to our new headquarters, but he felt that relocation to Chicago would not be in the best interest of his family.

- A true professional, [your name] is an indispensable asset to any organization. His team leadership skills, together with his visionary expertise, are unparalleled. Please feel free to contact me personally should you require any further information.

- I have worked with [you] for over eight years. There is no greater team player when it comes to any type of management. He listens to all parties concerned, sees the big picture, and has the confidence and foresight to integrate everyone's ideas to come up with a comprehensive plan that works for the company. He will sacrifice his own beliefs when it comes to the good of the company. However, that does not often happen because he has such an exacting pulse on the industry specifically and in economics and business in general.

- I was hired by [you] in 1983. Of the 12 interviews I went on, [your name] was the most professional, trustworthy,

➥

and honest hiring manager I encountered. He explained to me the pros and the cons of the job, and explicitly stated what he expected short- and long-term. He also clearly noted that he was there to train, develop, and coach us all to success.

- Apollo Dreams began operations in 1962 with zero sales. We had a new marketing concept that was different from anything existing on the market at that time. Most people resist change—not [your name]. He listened to our ideas, added some of his own, and, as a result was instrumental in assisting Apollo to its current market position as a $43 million company poised to go international and positioned for explosive growth.

- At a time when [you] could have enjoyed the relationships [you] had with other firms, [you] saw maintaining those relations was important while opening new markets. [You] got the president of his company to look at our program, negotiated a highly profitable arrangement for Vicene Horizontal, and gave us a chance. Today we sell over $3 million of our product, and [you] gave us credibility in the market.

- [You] saw the benefit to his customer and his company. He is a man of his word, a man of integrity, and a bottom-line progressive management professional. He helped make Stanford Designs what it is today and where it will go tomorrow. Anyone who hires him is truly fortunate to experience his professionalism.

Requesting Career Advice

- I am writing to ask your advice about careers in the consumer products industry. John Smith told me you have really enjoyed your career at PepsiCo and I would love to get some industry advice from you.

- I need your advice regarding whether I should take a position in management or stay in sales. Since you can view me objectively, your insight would very valuable.

- John, Pamela Alts suggested I contact you. She shared with me the growth you and your company have experienced the past three years and, knowing me, thought I would be a good fit in that industry. I am not asking to meet with you about a current position with your company, but merely want to get some advice and learn more about the g-nome business. I will call you Thursday to try to get on your calendar.

- Michael, I know I have not worked for you in several years, but I need some advice. You know me professionally as well as anyone. I am considering a career change, from the health-care field to, of all things, managing a furniture store. Can we schedule 15 to 20 minutes to talk so I can get your advice?

- Since you have successfully changed your profession, I am hoping you can give me some advice on a career change. I understand you went through a successful career change two years ago and it has worked out well for you. Maybe it's time I leave this company too and get a fresh start. I'd love your opinion on it.

- John, I know you hate giving advice, but I need your experience on my side. I have the opportunity to buy out another fisherman's fleet at the end of the season. The trouble is,

➡

this will put us in a real bind financially next season. I hope you will come on down. I will take you to lunch and we can look at the numbers together. I trust your judgment more than my own. I look forward to hearing from you.

- Jane, you are the one person I feel I can consult on this. I just got an opportunity to move to a competitor within the same industry. It represents a management, responsibility, and salary increase, but also involves a higher risk venture. I have been at Concorp for seven years and have a lot of stability in my position, 401K and vacation time, etc., and am not sure if I should take the risk. May we get together over lunch this week to discuss the opportunity and your thoughts?

- Greg, I am coming to you seeking advice on a personal matter because you have known me since college and I admire your life experiences and how your career has developed at Ford. I know also that you will honor my request for confidentiality.

- I need your advice. You are a friend who seems to know the right things to do in managing your career. I have taken a more passive approach and decided to take my career into my own hands and develop a plan. I'd love to speak to you directly about this rather than go into detail in a letter. Could we get together sometime next week to discuss my situation? I'll give you a call in the next few days to set a time. Thanks in advance for your time.

- Thanks so much for the advice you offered last week. Those who learn from others' experience are usually a step ahead of the rest. I am going to take your advice and pursue another opportunity. I believe you are correct in your assessment that sometimes you need to change companies in order to get ahead.

Resignation

Over my career to date, I have resigned from four different positions. Now, everyone, especially when you are more junior in your career, dreams of walking out or leaving your previous manager, if you did not like them or the company, with short notice to pay them back for any mistreatment they may have felt.

Don't EVER do that. At each one of my resignations, I left with as much class as when I started. One, it is the right thing to do, and two, a poor exit can erase years of hard work. It is the lasting impression. If you leave with as much commitment as normal, your peers and management will marvel at your commitment and professionalism. If you start coming in late, leaving early, blowing off tasks, or leave with short notice, it will be your legacy.

Some brief tips:
- Prepare your resignation: Remove your personal items from your office, clean up your computer files (leave any important work files with guides to where they are), try to wrap up any key projects.
- Give proper notice. They may not accept two weeks, but offer it.
- Offer to help train a replacement or help recruit a replacement.
- Ask for a letter of recommendation. This may ensure a good reference if needed later.
- Say good-bye with class. No negative comments as you walk out the door.

Perfect Phrases for Resigning

- This is to inform you that an opportunity has presented itself that will enable me to work in the area of my stated preference. Therefore, I am tendering my resignation from your company. The last day of my employment will be two weeks from today, May 23, 20__. At that time I shall deliver all property of the firm in my possession. Thank you for the experience of having worked for D&G, a truly outstanding organization.

- I am sorry to inform you that circumstances dictate I must resign from my position as Division Manager. I will gladly comply with the company's request to give two weeks termination notice.

- Each year my financial obligations have increased; unfortunately, my salary here has not been able to keep up with these demands. As a result, I have been forced to reconsider my employment here and have concluded that it would be best for me to seek an employment opportunity to better meet my financial requirements. It is with mixed emotions that I have accepted a position elsewhere that carries a higher salary with possibilities for future advancement. Please accept my thanks for the opportunity to work with you. The guidance you have given me has proved invaluable and has prepared me well for my new position. I have enjoyed the challenges presented here at Doe's, and I sincerely hope that I have returned adequate service for all the benefits that I have received.

- I would be happy to help you find and train a suitable replacement. Because my projects are current and because I have left detailed instructions illustrating ➡

how to perform my job duties on my desk, my successor should have little difficulty assuming my responsibilities. Please let me know if there is anything else I can do to help make this a smooth transition.

- Please accept my regrets in resigning from my position as Marketing Manager, effective two weeks from today's date. Eager to pursue new challenges, I have decided to accept a job offer in a field more closely aligned with my course of study. My new position will put my talents and interests to work in a new and exciting area. Although I have accepted a position in another field, it does not detract from the fact that my job at AT&T has provided me pleasure as well as insight into my hopes for the future. I have enjoyed working with all of my friends here, and I want to thank everyone for their support over the years. When my resignation date arrives, I expect all my projects to be current and my obligations fulfilled. If there is anything else I can do to help make this a smooth transition, please let me know.

- Please accept this letter as official notification of my resignation from my position as Floor Manager, effective immediately. Financial considerations and a desire to further my career compel me to accept a job offer from a company that is better able to fill my present needs. Although I am disappointed that size constraints placed upon the company deny rapid upward mobility, I feel deeply indebted to you for skills I have acquired and experience I have gained. My job here has been a great source of personal satisfaction and a foundation from which I have cultivated many irreplaceable ties with coworkers.

➡

- My last day of being a manager at Square D will be two weeks from Friday, as I am resigning to accept another position. I have been offered a Human Resource position and I am anxious to make a career change. I will, however, be happy to answer any questions or concerns the new manager may have, regardless of where I am employed. Thank you for all you have done for me. I appreciate the opportunities and friendships I have enjoyed here.

- Regretfully, I must inform you that I need to resign from my position here as office manager. In accordance with company policy, I am offering two weeks notice, effective today. Please know that I am grateful for the trust and confidence that you have placed in me in the last three years. I especially appreciated the opportunity to convert the paper files in the order department to a computerized system. I believe that similar conversions in other departments, though time-consuming in the beginning, would greatly benefit the company in the long run.

- I have been offered a position as Technology Specialist in a larger company and I feel I must accept. Although the higher salary was one factor in my decision, I will also have a greater opportunity to use my degree in computer science. Of course, I will be happy to help train a replacement while I am here. The new manager is also free to call me at home or e-mail me with any questions after I leave. All of my files have been backed up on CD-R and are labeled appropriately. Please let me know if there is anything else I can do to help make this transition as trouble free as possible.

Thank-You Letters

Don't underestimate the power of a thank-you letter. Immediately after a round of interviews, always send a thank-you letter to each of your interviewers by fax, mail, or e-mail.

E-mail is the quickest way to get thank-you letters in front of interviewers, and is perfectly acceptable these days. But avoid using cutesy Net stuff, like emoticons (e.g., happy faces), shorthand and acronyms (e.g., *u* for "you" and *TIA* for "thanks in advance"). Regardless of how you send them, follow professional, business letter standards. Near the end of your interviews, ask each interviewer for his or her contact information and correct name spelling, or just ask for a business card.

Most interviewers expect you to send thank-you letters. It's also an effective interviewing strategy. For example, it:

- Shows that you are courteous, knowledgeable, and professional
- Demonstrates your written communication skills, so make sure you double-proof it and read it aloud before sending
- Helps to make you stand out in the minds of the interviewers
- Elevates you above competing candidates who didn't bother to write them
- Gives you an opportunity to reinforce your good points
- Allows you to include something important you forgot to mention during your interview
- Confirms your understanding of topics discussed and helps to avoid misunderstandings

When sending a thank-you letter to the hiring manager or recruiter, it is important to lead with a section restating your understanding of their needs: what success in this position means to them. Then you want to quickly review that your skills and experience match their needs. Then let them know of your interest and when you will contact them to follow up.

When sending would-be peers a thank-you note, make it briefer. Thank them for their time, recall a comment from the interview, and mention that you would welcome the opportunity to work with them. Then sign off.

Perfect Phrases for Thank-You Letters

- Thank you for scheduling my interviews for the engineering manager opportunity. I am pleased with the benefits Lockheed offers and impressed with its long-term outlook and programs in the works. I'd greatly appreciate the chance to contribute to its future success. After completing my interviews today, I am confident that my qualifications are in line with your requirements. As promised, I will fax my completed job application to you by tomorrow afternoon. I've double-checked with my references and they are all available to talk with you.
- Thank you for taking the time to discuss employment opportunities at GMC with me.
- I appreciate your courtesy and the time you took to answer my questions during my visit this morning.
- Thank you for the pleasant interview we had on Monday. You were very helpful in explaining the job requirements.
- Thank you for meeting with me yesterday. I appreciate your insights and advice.
- I appreciated our meeting in your office yesterday and found the interview very informative.

- Thank you for the time and courtesy you extended to me at our interview this morning.
- Meeting with you yesterday was a pleasure. I appreciate the time you took out of your busy schedule as well as the information you gave me.
- Thank you for giving me the opportunity to learn more about the management position currently available at the Platery plant.
- I appreciate the time you took yesterday to discuss the possibility of my becoming the head nurse at Columbia Health Center.
- Thank you for meeting with me today to discuss the new opportunity in your group. What CFW is doing in the new consumer markets space is indeed exciting. To successfully launch the new campaign, you will likely need someone experienced at marketing and distribution. As I mentioned in our interview, I led the team that successfully launched Frito-Lays new Star Wars campaign …
- Thank you for taking the time to interview me yesterday for the Department Secretary position. You emphasized that managing multiple projects simultaneously and attention to detail are critical needs for you. I learned a great deal about multitasking as a partner's legal secretary as well as the importance of accuracy in my work. I believe I could work well with your faculty and staff; in fact, it would be a pleasure to work with them. I will call you Friday to speak with you in more detail about the position.
- I appreciate the opportunity I had yesterday to interview with you. Our meeting reminded me of the reason I first

considered your company for employment, namely, your reputation for friendly service. I believe that in today's competitive market it is friendly service that gives a competitive edge in keeping customers coming back. I gained that conviction during experience in public relations with the FGH Corporation. If hired, I promise to uphold your company's reputation for friendly, efficient service. I look forward to hearing from you.

- It was kind of you to meet with me this afternoon to discuss the group manager opportunity with Nokia. As we discussed your objectives and my background, it became clear that my knowledge, skills, and work experience have prepared me well to join your Programming Department. It would be a pleasure to work among such giants in the industry. I am certain I can replicate the success I realized at HP within your group at Nokia.

- Thanks so much for taking the time to speak with me this morning. I am very excited about the merger between Compaq and HP and the leadership position the new company will serve in the consumer space. Having managed the PR for the AWS/Cingular merger, my experience merging two technical industry giants will lend valuable experience in anticipating challenges and Wall Street perceptions as you merge these two brands and organizations.

- Thank you for interviewing me for the position of executive secretary. Because of the four years experience I have as an executive secretary, I feel I am well-suited for the job. You will find me extremely reliable, as I encourage you to follow up with my current manager.

➡

I have had a terrific tenure supporting my director, but need to leave since my husband is relocating with his position to Dallas. I am very encouraged by the new products DSC is launching and would love to join your team.

- I am grateful to you for taking time yesterday to meet with me. Our interview answered many questions I had about the position and what you need to be successful. Happily, I now feel I am even better suited to the job than I had anticipated. My experience overseas has prepared me for the challenges of managing international transfers for Ford. The prospect of my association with your firm is very exciting. In addition to rewarding work and an excellent benefits package, Ford's reputation is unsurpassed.

Additional Resources

Action Verbs Used in Cover Letters

Action verbs should be used abundantly throughout your cover letters to promote your achievements, to represent you as action-oriented and make your cover letter or résumé answer the question, "So what?" when it comes to your accomplishments.

**Communication/
People Skills**

Addressed	Conveyed	Incorporated
Advertised	Convinced	Influenced
Arbitrated	Corresponded	Interacted
Arranged	Debated	Interpreted
Articulated	Defined	Interviewed
Authored	Developed	Involved
Clarified	Directed	Joined
Collaborated	Discussed	Judged
Communicated	Drafted	Lectured
Composed	Edited	Listened
Condensed	Elicited	Marketed
Conferred	Enlisted	Mediated
Consulted	Explained	Moderated
Contacted	Expressed	Negotiated
	Formulated	Observed
	Furnished	Outlined

Participated
Persuaded
Presented
Promoted
Proposed
Publicized
Reconciled
Recruited
Referred
Reinforced
Reported
Resolved
Responded
Solicited
Specified
Spoke
Suggested
Summarized
Synthesized
Translated
Wrote

Creative Skills

Acted
Adapted
Began
Combined
Composed
Conceptualized

Condensed
Created
Customized
Designed
Developed
Directed
Displayed
Drew
Entertained
Established
Fashioned
Formulated
Founded
Illustrated
Initiated
Instituted
Integrated
Introduced
Invented
Modeled
Modified
Originated
Performed
Photographed
Planned
Revised
Revitalized
Shaped
Solved

Accounting/ Financial Skills

Administered
Adjusted
Allocated
Analyzed
Appraised
Assessed
Audited
Balanced
Budgeted
Calculated
Computed
Conserved
Corrected
Determined
Developed
Estimated
Forecasted
Managed
Marketed
Measured
Netted
Planned
Prepared
Programmed
Projected
Qualified
Reconciled

Additional Resources

Reduced
Researched
Retrieved

Team Support Skills

Adapted
Advocated
Aided
Answered
Arranged
Assessed
Assisted
Clarified
Coached
Collaborated
Contributed
Cooperated
Counseled
Demonstrated
Diagnosed
Educated
Encouraged
Ensured
Expedited
Facilitated
Familiarized
Furthered
Guided

Helped
Insured
Intervened
Motivated
Prevented
Provided
Referred
Rehabilitated
Represented
Resolved
Simplified
Supplied
Supported
Volunteered

Management/ Leadership Skills

Administered
Analyzed
Appointed
Approved
Assigned
Attained
Authorized
Chaired
Considered
Consolidated
Contracted
Controlled

Converted
Coordinated
Decided
Delegated
Developed
Directed
Eliminated
Emphasized
Enforced
Enhanced
Established
Executed
Generated
Handled
Headed
Hired
Hosted
Improved
Incorporated
Increased
Initiated
Inspected
Instituted
Led
Managed
Merged
Motivated
Navigated
Organized

Originated
Overhauled
Oversaw
Planned
Presided
Prioritized
Produced
Recommended
Reorganized
Replaced
Restored
Reviewed
Scheduled
Secured
Selected
Streamlined
Strengthened
Supervised
Terminated

Organizational Skills

Approved
Arranged
Catalogued
Categorized
Charted
Classified
Coded
Collected

Compiled
Corrected
Corresponded
Distributed
Executed
Filed
Generated
Incorporated
Inspected
Logged
Maintained
Monitored
Obtained
Operated
Ordered
Organized
Prepared
Processed
Provided
Purchased
Recorded
Registered
Reserved
Responded
Reviewed
Routed
Scheduled
Screened
Submitted
Supplied

Standardized
Systematized
Updated
Validated
Verified

Analytical Skills

Analyzed
Clarified
Collected
Compared
Conducted
Critiqued
Detected
Determined
Diagnosed
Evaluated
Examined
Experimented
Explored
Extracted
Formulated
Gathered
Inspected
Interviewed
Invented
Investigated
Located
Measured

Additional Resources

Organized
Researched
Reviewed
Searched
Solved
Summarized
Surveyed
Systematized
Tested
Coaching/Teaching
Skills
Adapted
Advised
Clarified
Coached
Communicated
Conducted
Coordinated
Critiqued
Developed
Enabled
Encouraged
Evaluated
Explained
Facilitated
Focused
Guided
Individualized
Informed
Instilled

Instructed
Motivated
Persuaded
Simulated
Stimulated
Taught
Tested
Trained
Transmitted
Tutored

Technical Skills

Adapted
Applied
Assembled
Built
Calculated
Computed
Conserved
Constructed
Converted
Debugged
Designed
Determined
Developed
Engineered
Fabricated
Fortified
Installed

Maintained
Operated
Overhauled
Printed
Programmed
Rectified
Regulated
Remodeled
Repaired
Replaced
Restored
Solved
Specialized
Standardized
Studied
Upgraded
Utilized